JAMES ROBINSON
JOHNSTON

NIMBUS
PUBLISHING LTD

THE LIFE, DEATH AND LEGACY
OF NOVA SCOTIA'S FIRST BLACK LAWYER

JUSTIN MARCUS JOHNSTON

Nimbus Publishing Limited
PO Box 9166
Halifax, NS   B3K 5M8
(902) 455-4286

Printed and bound in Canada

Design: Kathy Kaulbach, Paragon Design Group

Library and Archives Canada Cataloguing in Publication

>   Johnston, Justin, 1980-
>   James Robinson Johnston : the life, death, and legacy
>   of Nova Scotia's first black lawyer / Justin Johnston.
>
>   Includes bibliographical references.
>   ISBN 1-55109-509-2

1. Johnston, James Robinson, 1876-1915. 2. Lawyers—Nova Scotia—Biography.
3. Black Canadians—Nova Scotia-Biography. I. Title.

KE416.J64J64 2005   340'.092   C2004-907210-2   KF345.Z9J64 J64 2005

We acknowledge the financial support of the Government of Canada through
the Book Publishing Industry Development Program (BPIDP) and the Canada
Council for our publishing activities.

THIS BOOK IS DEDICATED to my late mother, Ethel May Gladys Johnston, and late grandmother Esther Pearl Johnston, whose inspiration and encouragement have provided the basis for this book.

FOREWORD

THE JAMES ROBINSON JOHNSTON CHAIR in Black
Canadian Studies at Dalhousie University, Halifax, Nova
Scotia, established in 1991, is a unique senior academic post
in Canada. It is national and based in Halifax in recognition of
the unique historical presence of Black people in the area. The
goal of the post is to serve as a centre of excellence in Black
Canadian scholarship, to coordinate national and international
conferences, and to serve as a crucible for the development
of scholars in Black Canadian studies. The uniqueness of the
post is that the work programme of the Chair is shaped by
the concerns of a particular set of constituencies who identify
themselves as Black of African descent; they have a major role
in making the Chair accountable to such communities.

It is strange that such an important academic position
is named in honour of a man about whom very little is
known, even in his home city of Halifax, Nova Scotia. The
biography by Justin Robinson Johnston attempts to redress
this dearth of knowledge by accessing hitherto unknown
family archives. What has resulted is the most complete
picture to date of this man. James Robinson Johnston: The
Life, Death and Legacy of Nova Scotia's First Black Lawyer
chronicles the key events in his life, family origins, educational
history, professional milestones, church involvement, wider
community participation and emerging political aspirations.
It also highlights how significant and powerful white leaders
in the wider community assisted Johnston in his struggle

towards prominence. We now know through this book more about "Lawyer Johnston," but are we nearer to understanding the man himself? The answer in my view is no and alas this is likely to remain the case. What was James Robinson Johnston like as a person? What motivated him to work so hard in a segregated education system to become the first indigenous Black law graduate from Dalhousie University? Why was he singled out by rich white patrons and why were pathways cleared facilitating his progress? Why was he so committed to working to advance his fellow Black community members, investing so much of his time and efforts, often at great personal and professional cost? A favourable, influential, and comfortable family background, a tradition of family community involvement and a sense of family obligations only partly answer such questions.

What were the real reasons for his brutal, untimely death a few days short of his thirty-ninth birthday by a family member? And why, after some ten thousand people turned up to his funeral, was he consigned to oblivion shortly afterwards by the very people who he appeared to represent tirelessly during his short life? One gets a strong feeling of being short-changed by what recorded information has been left about James Robinson Johnston. This may be the result of him having lived such a short life, or perhaps he did not have the time or the energy to leave the necessary paper trail for future biographers to follow. It may be also that decisions were taken to ensure that as little information as possible was made available about this man after his death, thus helping the process of community memory loss. Who knows?

I have a great deal of sympathy for Lawyer Johnston. He was a Black man living in a dire time trying to make a name for himself and at the same time acknowledging a fact often unheeded by some conventionally successful Black people: by virtue of his success and position, he had an obligation to assist others less fortunate than himself. He was a conscious Black man, aware of his history, the position of Black people at the time in a deeply racist society, cognizant of the reality that if one is to redress inequity then one needs allies from across the racial and cultural divides and that one must strive to occupy positions of influence and be equipped to handle those competently once they've been gained. Johnston also knew that members of the Black communities needed to have additional skills and educational opportunities to participate effectively in a radically changing environment. He not only identified such needs, but also sought with allies to have those needs met. The legacy lives on to this day.

He was radical. He was ahead of his time. He was human. He tried. This book by Justin Marcus Johnston is a welcome addition to bringing the memory of Lawyer Johnston to a wider audience and it is to be commended.

Professor David Divine
James Robinson Johnston Chair in Black Canadian Studies
Dalhousie University, Halifax
December 2004

Preface

NINETY YEARS AGO Nova Scotia's principal black leader was struck down, just days before his thirty-ninth birthday. Though many have heard of the James Robinson Johnston Chair in Black Canadian Studies at Dalhousie University, few are really familiar with the life and times of this important man. It has been my personal quest as biographer and descendant to really understand who James Robinson Johnston was and reclaim his name. His story is not just a personal one—it is the story of a family and an entire community.

I first became interested in James Robinson Johnston during my childhood. My grandparents told me stories about a famous lawyer in the family who died in a quarrel many years ago. At university, I pursued a degree in history, and it was then that I decided to start research on my great-great grand-uncle, his life and his legacy.

Early on, I learned that the circumstances and events that led to Johnston's murder have been subject to innuendo and debate within and outside of the black community for many years. Few people have wanted to speak publicly about how he met his end. Consequently, many details of his life and death have been suppressed by my family and the broader black community. Attempts have been made to tell Johnston's story, but these often present incomplete and inaccurate, sometimes even prejudicial, information. None—until now—have been written from within the family.

Learning about Johnston's life has allowed me to learn more about my own past. Despite not having known the people whose stories I tell in this book, I feel that I have become closer to them in spirit.

James R. Johnston's struggle to become a lawyer in Nova Scotia in the late 1890s is symbolic of the struggle black Nova Scotians have faced over the centuries in overcoming slavery and the more insidious, entrenched barriers of racism. In this, it is a story for us all.

Justin Marcus Johnston
October, 2004

Table of Contents

Lawyer Johnston's Defence

Please remember what's been proved:
I played no Sambo or Uncle Tom;
Neither burnt-cork nor white powder disgraced my face.

I come up by way of Gerrish, Creighton, y'all,
And Gotti'gen Street:
Another Haligonian intellectual from the 'hood—
Un frére philosophe—
Who tapped Ecclesiastes to zap Plato.

I got to Dal and got my letters—
B.L., LL.B:
Was that a crime?

I learned how to talk:
I learned how to talk back—
Hear me, good people—
To judges and cops.
So when George V was but a prince,
I was the one of us chosen—
In my black top hat, black coat, and white gloves—
To represent us Coloured (Baptist) Scotians
To the dandy throne of England.

I didn't tomcat around or peacock about;
I didn't do monkeyshines at *soirées,*
Or spread bull from pulpits,
Or spew venom *in camera.*

True: the public credits lawyers
As shysters, swindlers, chisellers,
Living for the music of jewelled clapping,
Or dining off of people's tears.

But I died intestate,
With only stony potato patches to my name:
My poor widow had to scrub floors in Montreal.
One of my learnèd colleagues became Prime Minister;
I only got to minister to worms.

      You jurors who wear second-hand shoes
Will appreciate that, in my time,
Coloured chaps who wrote Latin and spoke Greek
Polished shoes and handed out towels in men's rooms.
So when I answered the call
To lawyer,
I knew my duty:
To sobre and save the "unsavoury";
To back the lowly vs. lofty muck-a-mucks;
To salvage indigent, unlettered drunks accused of homicide;
And to circuit Nova Scotia everywhichway like—
Pardon me—an apostle.
(Mustn't anyone meaning to be upright
get down with the strivers,
the downtrodden,
to do that *heavy* uplifting?)

      Friends, I hope you might remember
How I, too, liked my jollification, sure.
With the Coloured People's Celebration Committee
(kinda like your Central Planning Committee
75 years later),
I mingled politics with pleasure—
Because a *party* should also be a party:
Even Tories danced at Cana, eh?

      Citizens, when those alcoholic, persnickety Grits
Got all keyed up, whiskey'd up,

Busted into the Preston schoolhouse
To havoc and dismay our Negro pupils,
I jumped into the papers and hurled shame
On their shenanigans—
I howled like Ol' Joe Howe, that tribune—
So those scalawags never ruckus'd again.

      Okay, my time is up. I know.
I'm gonna rest this defence and go back to my rest.
But, allow me to say this much
About the trial of the "brother"
Who shot me in the mouth,
Stopping what truth I could tell:
Gossip—hogwash, pig sauce—
Be trivial vitriol.
If ever I did abuse my bright-skinned beaut of a bride,
Well, my God did chide and chastise me.
And if my cool killer was really my assassin,
See how he croaked from his rat-bite rabies,
Stinking, messing his pants, crazed.

      I do regret my reputation was filched—filthied—
By strutting, tut-tutting hypocrites.
But those without *grit* can't have *integrity*.

      Please forgive me, though, for noticing,
In scripture as in history,
That prophesying dreamers strive
Always against slander,
Then poison, knives, bullets:
Backward-stumbling people hate anyone inching forward.

George Elliott Clarke
University of Toronto
December IV

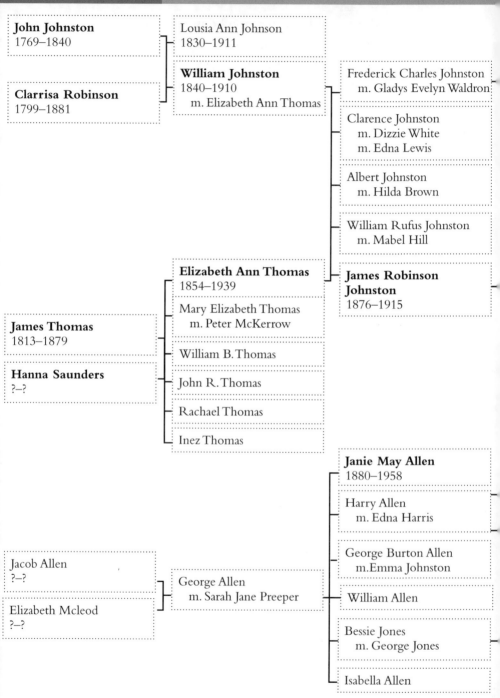

John Johnston
1769–1840

Clarrisa Robinson
1799–1881

Lousia Ann Johnson
1830–1911

William Johnston
1840–1910
   m. Elizabeth Ann Thomas

Frederick Charles Johnston
m. Gladys Evelyn Waldron

Clarence Johnston
m. Dizzie White
m. Edna Lewis

Albert Johnston
m. Hilda Brown

William Rufus Johnston
m. Mabel Hill

Elizabeth Ann Thomas
1854–1939

Mary Elizabeth Thomas
m. Peter McKerrow

**James Robinson
Johnston**
1876–1915

James Thomas
1813–1879

Hanna Saunders
?–?

William B. Thomas

John R. Thomas

Rachael Thomas

Inez Thomas

Janie May Allen
1880–1958

Harry Allen
m. Edna Harris

George Burton Allen
m. Emma Johnston

Jacob Allen
?–?

Elizabeth Mcleod
?–?

George Allen
m. Sarah Jane Preeper

William Allen

Bessie Jones
m. George Jones

Isabella Allen

Gerald Johnston
1927–
    m. Esther Pearl Lappie

Ethel May Gladys Johnston
1959–1998

Justin Marcus Johnston
1980–

George Henry Stanton
1910–1911

William Allen
1935–

Francis A. W. Jones
    m. Philomena Amos

Robert "Buddy" Jones
1925–

James Robinson Johnston / c.1890
Halifax Academy Photo

INTRODUCTION

JAMES ROBINSON JOHNSTON (1876–1915) was one of a kind. Among the most important black leaders Canada has yet to produce, ninety years after his death he has been forgotten. In view of Johnston's many achievements towards black advancement in early twentieth century Nova Scotia, it is remarkable that his name is so little known today. Why hasn't James R. Johnston become a symbol of black pride, and an example of the ability to overcome adversity? How can a person of such accomplishment and influence in his own lifetime be so disregarded after his death? Answering these difficult questions requires consideration of Johnston's own life, as well as reflection upon the historical climate of turn-of-the-century Nova Scotia, and the nuances of Halifax's black community. Johnston's lost legacy stems in part from the scandal associated with his death, but a widespread lack of African-Canadian historical consciousness is also to blame. Ninety years after his death, it is time for Johnston's name to be reclaimed. Though his character may have had flaws, and though the circumstances surrounding his untimely death will remain a mystery, Johnston is too important a figure in Nova Scotia's past to cancel him from history forever.

A pillar of the black establishment, "Lawyer Johnston," as he was known by his peers, was an Edwardian man of his time. Indeed he was the only member of Halifax's black community presented to His Royal Highness the Prince of Wales (afterwards King George V) during his two-day visit in October 1901.

Johnston was also a lawyer—the first black professional person in Nova Scotia—and a successful criminal defence counsel. It took great ambition for a black man of his time to become a lawyer, a position that in turn reinforced his status as a community leader. Further, he additionally influenced his community by being active in politics. Some say he might one day have entered government.

To cement his influence and power in the black community, Johnston was active in the African Baptist Church, as black community leaders customarily came from the church. He was involved in many other types of community organizations as well, both black and white, always working to foster social development and racial integration. Perhaps most importantly, Johnston was a strong advocate for formal education. He wanted there to be more black people like himself—highly educated, progressive, and influential—people who could make a concrete change in the structure and status of the black community.

Due to his extraordinary visions and drive to execute change within all avenues of the black community, Johnston had no equal or successor as a race leader. He also had no followers as a lawyer for nearly forty years. In 1952, an indigenous black bar was reborn when George Webber Roache Davis QC was called to the bar—but to this day there are relatively few native black Nova Scotian lawyers, by comparison with those from the West Indies. There are two black judges in Nova Scotia, but the glass ceiling has prevented any black lawyer or judge from being appointed or promoted to the Supreme Court or the Court of Appeal. The Indigenous Blacks and Mi'kmaq Program at Dalhousie Law School, established to address the problem, has been only partially successful, and in the late 1990s attention was drawn to the near-complete absence of black lawyers from Halifax's largest law firms. The neglected promise of James R. Johnston's life continues to cast a shadow over the fortunes of black lawyers in Nova Scotia.

Clearly, Johnston's position in the black community as an educated professional and an advocate for change indicates he was far ahead of his time. It is time to reclaim his memory, his accomplishments, and his aims for the black community, and bring them to life again. To do so, Johnston's accomplishments and the influence he had on his community need to be resurrected. For Johnston's successes to be celebrated, however, the black community must also heal from the painful consequences of his shocking murder. His death—and the memory of it—continues to haunt and shame his community. The complex issues surrounding his death and the manner of his demise undercut the endeavours of his life. Difficult as it may be to recover from the rift the scandal created, it is necessary to deal with the details of Johnston's brutal death, as well as give long overdue attention to his exceptional life.

Part I: Origins

JAMES R. JOHNSTON HAD THE PRIVILEGE of being born into an already influential family in Halifax's black community, giving him an early advantage. Tracing his ancestral roots provides perspective on how his family, as well as many others in Nova Scotia's black population, became established.

Early History of Blacks in Nova Scotia

When Halifax was founded in 1749, there were fewer than fifty blacks dispersed throughout Nova Scotia, mostly slaves who were located at Annapolis Royal. By 1767, immigration out of New England caused the population of free black Nova Scotians to grow to just over a hundred, out of the total provincial population of 13,374. The next twenty years would see two major influxes of black settlers: the freed blacks from America and the Maroons from Jamaica. Scottish immigration correlated roughly with black immigration; however, because the Scots did not face barriers of racial discrimination, they were able to thrive, despite their humble beginnings, whereas the black immigrants faced segregation and settlement under government control.

In 1775, the thirteen colonies of America rose up against Great Britain's rule. Those in the colonies who did not want to fight against Britain—the Loyalists—fled to Canada. Blacks were offered freedom from slavery in Canada by Britain.

Subsequently, about one in ten refugees to reach Nova Scotia was black.

The Maroons were free blacks from Jamaica who had struggled for independence from colonial rule. A treaty of peace between the British and Maroons signed in 1738 broke down in 1795, and about six hundred settlers came to Nova Scotia between the years 1796 to 1800, mainly to work for the military. However, the Maroons were treated poorly by the British, who saw them as little more than a convenient and cheap labour source. The paternalism and disrespect proud and independent Maroons encountered in Nova Scotia caused them to waste little time here. Most of them petitioned to be resettled to Africa, and were removed to Sierra Leone, another British colony.

A significant migration of blacks to Nova Scotia came after the War of 1812 between Britain and the United States, when about two thousand refugees came from the States between 1813 and 1816. Any slaves in the United States who fled their masters were promised free passage, land, and freedom by the British. Most of the black refugees came by ship from the Chesapeake Bay area in Maryland and Virginia to Preston, Hammond's Plains, Refugee Hill (now Beechville), and Halifax, in Nova Scotia. The former slaves were ill-received by the Nova Scotian government and the general population. Disease and poverty were widespread, and many white Nova Scotians tried to have the refugees relocated to another colony. Despite difficult conditions, however, the immigrants survived and clung to their settlements in the Preston area and elsewhere, mostly throughout Halifax County.

The experience of the early black settlers in Nova Scotia was not an easy one. Beset by discrimination and segregation, only their will to survive kept them rooted. Unsurprisingly, a strongly unified community took shape, and institutions such as church and school formed a sense of kinship which helped the early black settlers of Nova Scotia survive. These institutions only grew stronger with time and continued to play an integral role in black communities in the province. The church, in particular, was a common source of influential leaders in the black community.

THOMAS AND SAUNDERS FAMILY

Joseph and Sarah Thomas, and their three sons, came to Nova Scotia from Wales. James Thomas would have been about twelve years old. The names of James's brothers are not known. The family settled on a farm at Lake Eagle near present-day Preston. The exact year of the family's arrival cannot be established, nor can their exact reasons for coming to Nova Scotia. However, according to oral tradition, Sarah Thomas was Jewish. This fact might have prompted the couple's emigration, as Jewish merchants would have been persecuted in Wales in this period, and a mixed (Gentile/Jew) marriage would have meant total ostracization for the couple. Emigration to the colonies might have been the only alternative, as their livelihood and perhaps even their lives may have been at risk.

Joseph and Sarah Thomas, both white, operated a fur business, and frequently travelled to Halifax on account of it. Joseph Thomas was a hatter and furrier—a skilled craftsman who eventually set up shop in the city in order to retail to clients who could afford fur hats, stoles, and other fine fur products. Joseph Thomas died on April 28, 1833; the date of Sarah Thomas's death is not known. Following his parents' deaths, James Thomas continued the business, operating a large fur shop called "Thomas & Company," which was located on the corner of Barrington and Sackville streets. The shop remained in the family until 1894.

James Thomas joined the African Baptist Church and married Hanna Saunders, a black woman from Preston. Little is known about Hanna's background, though she was likely the daughter of refugee blacks who settled in the Preston area. The couple had six children: William B., John R., Elizabeth Ann, Mary Elizabeth, Inez, and Rachel.

By the 1870s, the Thomas family had become leaders among African Nova Scotians. Their standing derived from James Thomas's role as protégé of Richard Preston and his eighteen-year pastorate of the "mother church" (Cornwallis Street Baptist Church) and moderatorship of the African Baptist Association (ABA). James Thomas succeeded Richard Preston as patriarch of the black community, entrenching his authority and prestige by marrying a black woman. This was decisive—under slavery, social negritude descended through the black mother. (African Diaspora families and their descendants are matriarchal, so the child assumes the racial identity of the mother.) Moreover, the Thomas family had, over the years, continued to produce and associate with many prominent leaders in the African Nova Scotian community, such as Peter E. Mackerrow, an Antiguan by birth who married James Thomas's oldest daughter, Mary Elizabeth, and who was a long-term clerk of the ABA. Mackerrow supported Thomas politically.

REV. RICHARD PRESTON AND THE AFRICAN BAPTIST CHURCH

Richard Preston was an escaped slave from Virginia who came to Halifax in 1816, as part of the refugee migration after the war of 1812, in search of his mother. He eventually found her in the township of Preston, after which he took his name. Preston was a gifted orator and in 1823 became a preacher, initially without any formal theological training. In his day, he was known as "Father Preston." The term "Father" or "Black Father" was used to describe black preachers who were former slaves or who preached without formal ministerial training.

With the help of Rev. John Burton, who established the first Baptist church in Halifax some years before, and other Baptist leaders, Richard Preston went to England to study. On May 8, 1832, the West London Baptist Association ordained him. While in England, Preston met many leading abolitionists, men like William Wilberforce and Thomas Buxton. While there, he petitioned for money to build a black Baptist church in Halifax and received £650 for the project. From this money, Cornwallis Street Baptist Church was born, with Richard Preston as the first pastor. Preston was a powerful force, establishing churches in every county between Halifax and the western edge of Nova Scotia.

On September 1, 1854, under Preston's leadership, black Baptist churches from across Nova Scotia united to form the African Baptist Association. The first order of business was to designate Cornwallis Street Baptist Church the "mother church" in the association. The establishment of the Cornwallis Street church and the African Baptist Association was Preston's great contribution to Nova Scotian history. To this day, Cornwallis Street Baptist Church remains the mother church of the ABA.

Preston died in 1861 and was succeeded by the Rev. James Thomas. Thomas had been ordained by Richard Preston in 1857, and was pastor of Cornwallis Street Baptist Church from 1861 to 1879, a period of great change. During this time, Thomas helped to enlarge the ABA, and was accepted by the white establishment. During his eighteen years as moderator, the association was faced with many challenges. A schism resulted when Rev. Benson Smithers, pastor of the

East Preston Baptist Church, withdrew from the association in 1869 and formed a separate association. Both Smithers and Thomas were prominent leaders in their day and competed among the faithful for adherents—the black community was divided and sides were taken. The exact cause of this conflict is difficult to determine, but the fact that Thomas was white may have been a contributing factor (Smithers was black). It was not until Thomas's death in 1879 that the ABA finally reunified.

Despite these challenges, Thomas was popular among many black Baptists, and was well known for his philanthropy. Shortly after his appointment as pastor in 1861, the church grew in need of repair. Thomas advanced the money with full confidence that the money would be repaid, which it was. Thomas's congregation were especially fond of his open-lake baptisms. Thomas purportedly holds the record for the most baptisms, at forty-seven immersions in twenty minutes at Beech Hill (now Beechville).

James Thomas died in 1879 after catching a cold during an open lake baptism. The funeral was held on June 12, 1879, at Cornwallis Street Baptist Church. Hanna Thomas remarried

THE **OPEN LAKE BAPTISM** IS AN OLD TRADITION IN AFRICAN AMERICAN RELIGIOUS CULTURE, ESPECIALLY IN RURAL AREAS. BAPTISMAL CANDIDATES DRESSED IN WHITE ROBES AND SANG SPIRITUALS WHILE WALKING FROM THE CHURCH TO A NEARBY LAKE OR POND. THEN, THE CLERGYMAN OFFERED A PRAYER BEFORE IMMERSING THE CANDIDATE IN "THE LIQUID STEAM." IT MAY BE DESCENDED FROM WEST AFRICAN BAPTISMAL PRACTICES.

in 1881, to John Colley of Preston, and is thought to have died in 1906, in her seventy-seventh year.

After Thomas's death in 1879, Rev. Alexander Bailey succeeded him as pastor of the Cornwallis Street Baptist Church. Bailey thus became responsible for this church, as well as the other, smaller churches in Halifax County.

The Thomas family connection would have a significant impact on subsequent generations of the family, particularly in relation to achievements and prominence in the black community. The Thomas surname is still associated with the present-day community of East Preston, Nova Scotia, where many of James Thomas's descendants remain.

THE JOHNSTON/ROBINSON FAMILY

John and Clarissa (Robinson) Johnston came to Nova Scotia as fugitive slaves after the War of 1812. According to oral tradition, John Johnston was born a slave in Virginia in about 1769. Family records show that Clarissa Robinson was born in 1799 in Liberty County, Georgia. John and Clarissa Johnston were among the refugees received by British forces at Chesapeake Bay and evacuated to Halifax. The date of John and Clarissa's marriage is not known.

John Johnston built and owned many of the homes on the street now called Gerrish Lane, and neighbouring streets in the north suburbs. Life for the Johnstons and their children would have revolved around the church and the family store, which were in close proximity to each other. John Johnston died shortly after the birth of his youngest son, William.

By 1838, Clarissa Johnston was a widow with four children, two boys and two girls. She later married John Smith, a shopkeeper in Halifax; the exact year of her remarriage is unknown. However, by the time of her death in 1881, she was again widowed, and the owner of a clothing and general store on the corner of Prince William and Gottingen streets. According to city of Halifax assessment records, the property, valued at £175 in 1834, remained in the Johnston family until 1917.

Of John and Clarissa's children, William and his older sister, Louisa Ann, were close. As the eldest, Louisa was her mother's favourite child. When Clarissa Johnston died in 1881, Louisa inherited the family store properties, and she and William established themselves as landlords.

Louisa Johnston married three times. Her second husband, Rev. Alexander Bailey, was the son of a slave and briefly held the pastorate of Cornwallis Street Baptist Church after the death of Rev. James Thomas in 1879. Louisa's final marriage was to George Washingston Tillman, a Baptist preacher from Boston, on February 4, 1911.

GERRISH LANE WAS ONCE CALLED GERRISH COURT AND LATER JOHNSTON LANE. THE PLACE OF JAMES'S BIRTH, IT LIES NESTLED BETWEEN GERRISH STREET TO THE NORTH AND GOTTINGEN STREET TO THE EAST. THE STREET NAME "GOTTINGEN" IS GERMAN AND ORIGINATED FROM GERMAN SETTLEMENT IN THE AREA SOON AFTER THE FOUNDING OF HALIFAX. THE SURROUNDING STREETS, WITH NAMES SUCH AS MAYNARD AND CREIGHTON, RECALL PROMINENT INDIVIDUALS IN THE EIGHTEENTH AND EARLY NINETEENTH CENTURIES. THE AREA WAS THE OLDEST COMMUNITY OF BLACKS IN THE CITY OF HALIFAX, LONG PREDATING FAMILIAR PLACES SUCH AS AFRICVILLE (FORMERLY KNOWN AS CAMPBELL ROAD SETTLEMENT).

Both William Johnston and Louisa Bailey were energetic leaders and influential in Halifax's black community. Bailey was a firm believer in women's rights and an active participant in the women's suffrage movement. She lived long enough to support the idea of a black industrial school being built in Halifax, and better education for blacks. Apart from supporting the women's movement and honing her entrepreneurial talents, Bailey was also active in the church community. She was involved in the African Baptist Association, attending its annual meetings as a delegate, and taught Sunday school at the Cornwallis Street Baptist Church. She died less than a year after her marriage to Tillman, on December 29, 1911. Upon her death, she generously bequeathed large sums of money to Cornwallis Street Baptist Church.

William Johnston was a cobbler, and for many years his shop and residence were at 131 Gottingen Street, a stone's throw from Gerrish Lane. By 1876, William moved from Gottingen Street to 5 Gerrish Lane. William was a deacon at Cornwallis Street Baptist Church, and a member of the Board of Trustees. Through his association with the church, he met Elizabeth Ann Thomas, the mulatto daughter of Rev. James Thomas and Hanna Saunders. (Mulatto means one parent was black and the other parent was white.) William and Elizabeth courted and were married on February 8, 1876, by the bride's father. At the time of the wedding, Elizabeth was eight months pregnant. Witnesses to the marriage were Elizabeth's sister, Mary Elizabeth, and her husband, Peter Evander Mackerrow (sometimes spelt McKerrow).

William Johnston, like his sister, was an influential figure in the black community; by marrying into the powerful Thomas family, William Johnston elevated his status further. Outspoken on the need for improved educational opportunities for blacks, he was respected by both blacks and whites. His influence in the community was evident prior to the 1897 election, as whites encouraged him to solicit nomination for city councillor in Ward 4, a predominantly black section of town. (He declined.) Moreover, Dr. John Forrest, president of Dalhousie College, was one of the officiants at Johnston's funeral. By the time of his death in 1910, William Johnston had become universally respected in both the black and white communities.

JAMES ROBINSON JOHNSTON

James Robinson Johnston was born to William and Elizabeth Johnston on March 12, 1876, at 5 Gerrish Lane. The Johnstons would have four more sons: William Rufus (1882), Albert (1888), Clarence (1892) and Frederick Charles (1898).

As a child, James was active in the community, especially so in the church, carrying on the family tradition. James joined the church in about 1886, at just ten years old, attending annual meetings of the ABA each summer as an observer. James's interest in the church at a young age was exceptional—at the time, few black youth belonged to the church.

James's ascent through the ranks of the ABA and Cornwallis Street Baptist Church was speeded through a combination of his natural abilities and the Thomas family connections in the African Baptist community. As well, his similarly quick ascent through the ranks of the educational system were clear indications to the black community that James Robinson Johnston was an exceptional young man full of promise.

PART II: LIFETIME ACHIEVEMENTS

THERE IS NO DOUBT that the Nova Scotia that James Robinson Johnston was born into was a highly racist society, with its powerful institutions and public perceptions directed primarily against blacks as a group. James Robinson Johnston and his family's position in the traditional institutions of church and community formed a pivotal foundation for their influence, as did their efforts to integrate black people into white society, to promote equal opportunities for all.

In the year of Johnston's birth in 1876, black youth were formally excluded from the city's public schools. The Liberal government of the time did nothing to change the status quo for blacks. Of course, the Liberal Party was probably no more or less racist than the Conservative (who had introduced the segregation provision in the first place). By 1883, the issue had become a political football; there had been an election in June 1882 in which the black-supported Conservative government was turfed out. Thus, the new Liberal government refused to amend the Education Act to repeal the offending provision. In addition, it was the former Liberal cabinet which had approved the request to segregate the public schools in Halifax, which suggests that the Liberals were at the very least in favour of colour-based segregation.

In 1883, a petition to end school segregation was spearheaded by black community leaders Peter Mackerrow and Rev. Alexander Bailey. The Education Act had been amended in 1865 by the Conservatives to allow for separate schools for blacks. Under the Liberals, who ruled from 1867 to 1878, requests to implement segregation were routinely granted. The timing of the petition had much to do with the return of the Liberals to government in 1882; blacks in Halifax, who suffered most from the provision, sought its repeal. The Liberals refused, while the Opposition Conservatives supported the blacks. The petition carried 106 signatures, with William Johnston's name near the top.

The black community was not willing to accept an inferior level of education. The 1883 petition called for an end to segregated schools in the city of Halifax so that blacks would receive the same educational opportunities as whites. In 1884, two years after Johnston entered the black Maynard School at age six, the Halifax board of school commissioners decided to allow blacks to attend white schools, provided they could pass the entrance examination conducted by the board supervisor. Due to the poor quality of their intra-community education, however, black students had difficulty passing these examinations. Of course, formal acceptance into a white school was only the first hurdle facing blacks: widespread racism added immense social and psychological barriers. Hence, despite the 1884 decision, education for blacks remained segregated. Because very few black students entered the white school system, the status quo remained firmly in place.

Fortunately for Johnston, he possessed a naturally keen intellect, as well as valuable family connections to help him navigate beyond institutional restrictions. In his early educational experiences at Maynard Street school, he was identified as an exceptionally bright student, often winning awards and prizes, as well as respect from his peers and teachers. People in the community began to take an interest in his future prospects.

Johnston's success in school brought him special permission from the county inspector of schools to write entrance exams for Albro Street, an exclusively white school. In 1887, he entered Albro Street, becoming the first black to attend a white school, post-segregation. A year later, he transferred to Halifax Academy, which was not segregated. Johnston finished his high school education in the spring of 1892.

James's academic perseverance paid off. In 1892, at age sixteen, an unusually young age for a first-year university student, he entered Dalhousie College (now university), becoming the first native African Nova Scotian to enter its doors.

Johnston's advancement was encouraged by Dr. John Forrest, a Presbyterian minister who stepped down from the pulpit in 1885 to become Dalhousie's third president. Forrest knew and admired William Johnston—he preached at his funeral in 1910, praising his respectability and standing in the community. Another likely supporter was Andrew Mitchell Uniacke, a wealthy Conservative philanthropist and friend of the black community. Uniacke was chair of the Halifax school board from 1866 to 1872, and would have been aware of Johnston's bright academic career. Without the active support of Forrest, Uniacke, and other influential patrons, Johnston might have been denied the opportunities withheld from black students in Nova Scotia at this time. Also, Dalhousie University was Presbyterian by tradition. Though few blacks were of that denomination, the Presbyterian Church in Canada was a staunch friend of the black community. It was a fortuitous combination of academic brilliance and powerful connections that paved the way for Johnston's acceptance at Dalhousie.

Johnston's experience as an undergraduate student was a busy and rewarding one. Upon entrance to Dalhousie College, he enrolled in the Bachelor of Letters program, which emphasized modern European languages, as opposed to a Bachelor of Arts, which emphasized classical Latin and Greek. He completed his first and second years successfully. In his third year Johnston developed an interest in law, and in 1894, he audited courses as a visiting student in the Faculty of Law. This interest may have been sparked by the on-campus presence of Trinidadian Henry Sylvester Williams, the first black to attend Dalhousie's law school, and later the founder of Pan-Africanism.

Details of what Johnston's life was like while studying for his degrees are sparse; most are available only through a few scattered newspaper clippings. One such account appears in the student newspaper, *Dalhousie Gazette*, shortly after his successful graduation from Dalhousie College with a Bachelor of Letters in 1896. Clearly, Johnston was a popular young man on campus, lively if somewhat restless, good-humoured, and with many friends:

Jimmie Johns[t]on loved notoriety and got it. He didn't aspire for classes, however, so in that field alone he missed his desire; but to this Halifax youth their phenomenal scarceness was perhaps a fame in itself. Jimmie had a silvery voice and a laugh that bubbled often and long upon the ears of the straining pluggers in the Arts library. He has entered upon the study of law and his fellows have offered a reward to any genius who has inventive powers enough to devise some means which may be successful in fixing Jimmie's attention upon one thing

PAN-AFRICANISM IS THE CONCEPT AND PROMOTION OF THE POLITICAL UNION OF ALL THE INDIGENOUS INHABITANTS OF AFRICA AND THE BLACK DIASPORA. IT INSPIRED THE BACK TO AFRICA MOVEMENT AND LED TO ANTI-COLONIALIST ACTIVISM IN BOTH BRITISH AFRICA AND THE BRITISH WEST INDIES.

and one person for a brief period per day. Long may he live to be the chosen pleader for his race in the police court of the city.

In 1896, Johnston entered Dalhousie's Faculty of Law as a degree student. Skillful at networking and always involved with community life, Johnston remained a popular student on campus. He participated in college activities, and served as secretary-treasurer of the Sodales Debating Club, one of the oldest student organizations on campus. Once again, the most revealing source of his time in law school comes from an article on his twenty-five-member graduating class from Dalhousie Law School, as chronicled in the *Dalhousie Gazette:*

[Johnston] was no unimportant member of this important class. His beaming face was always welcome amongst us. He had a particular

BY THE TIME OF JOHNSTON'S ARRIVAL AT DALHOUSIE IN THE FALL OF 1892, **EDWIN HOWARD BORDEN** HAD ALREADY BREACHED THE COLOUR BARRIER IN HIGHER EDUCATION. BORDEN WAS THE FIRST AFRICAN NOVA SCOTIAN GRADUATE OF ACADIA UNIVERSITY IN WOLFVILLE, NOVA SCOTIA. HE WAS BORN IN TRURO, AND RECEIVED HIS BACHELOR OF ARTS IN 1892, MASTER OF ARTS ALSO FROM ACADIA IN 1896, AND A BACHELOR OF DIVINITY FROM THE UNIVERSITY OF CHICAGO IN 1897. BORDEN LATER RECEIVED A PHD FROM MILTON UNIVERSITY, BALTIMORE, MARYLAND. **HENRY SYLVESTER WILLIAMS** (1869-1911) WAS BORN IN AROUCA, TRINIDAD. HE LATER MOVED TO CANADA TO OBTAIN HIGHER EDUCATION. HE ATTENDED DALHOUSIE LAW SCHOOL FROM 1893-94, AFTERWARDS BECOMING A SUCCESSFUL BARRISTER AND POLITICAL ACTIVIST.

fondness for the fair sex and in consequence always took a prominent part in the College "At Homes." Jimmie still shows a longing for Dalhousie, and he is taking the lectures in Procedure with us again. He will, we understand, put out his shingle in Halifax. He deserves great credit for the admirable way he has overcome obstacles to obtain a thorough preparation for the bar, and no doubt his untiring efforts will secure for him a prominent place in the future of our country.

Both newspaper accounts, though happy to tease Johnston, are also careful to make note of his future prospects, as well as his work for the advancement of the black community.

There is also record of Johnston's involvement with the "moot court." As a law student, Johnston conducted mock trials in the basement of Cornwallis Street Baptist Church. These were held during the second week of April 1898 and drew a large crowd from both the black and white communities. Though make-believe, the mock trials reinforced the idea that there would soon be a black lawyer to represent the community. Johnston served as the presiding judge, and the case on trial was *Matilda Thomas v. John Henpeck*. Fellow law classmates J. P. Foley represented the plaintiff, and Walter J. A. O'Hearn represented the defendant. The case involved a breach of promise suit in which Henpeck had allegedly promised to marry his girlfriend (Thomas), but changed his mind. First witness, Maltida Thomas, claimed that Henpeck had taken her to the egg pond and said that if she did not marry him, he would drown himself. On the stand, Henpeck admitted that he did court the plaintiff, but denied asking her to marry him. Within his testimony, however, he contradicted himself and the plaintiff went on to call Henpeck a thief and a perjurer. Henpeck responded to the plaintiff's lawyer by removing his coat and gesturing that he wanted to fight, but calmed down after noticing the sheriff in the courtroom. Counsel for the plaintiff and the judge addressed the jury, who made their decision, awarding $999.99 in damages to Matilda Thomas. The judge—Johnston—also ordered Henpeck to marry Thomas.

Beyond campus life, Johnston always remained strongly connected with the church community. He was energetic in his work with the church, becoming an officer of Cornwallis Street Baptist Church while working on his undergraduate degree. His involvement with Cornwallis Street Church was family tradition, as this was the church his grandfather was pastor of at the time of his birth. It is not known precisely when Johnston was baptized, but it would have been by 1895, at which time he acted as secretary for Cornwallis Street Baptist Church. A few years later in 1898, when he graduated from the Faculty of Law, Johnston served as president of the Baptist Young People's Union in the ABA, superintendent of the Sunday school, and a member of the finance committee. The following year, he proposed the appointment of a field missionary to travel to churches in the association, especially those in rural areas that had trouble keeping a pastor. Clearly, Johnston was skillful at balancing his studies and his work for the church.

Even the tight-knit community of the church, however, experienced discord. One problem the church had while Johnston was an officer involved the American expatriate minister Reverend Dr. J. Francis Robinson, who pastored briefly at Cornwallis Street in 1898. During a fundraising campaign in 1898, distinguished speakers from the United States were invited to come to the church in hopes of raising money. Rev. Dr. George Claude Lorimer was pastor at Tremont Temple Baptist Church in Boston, and George Henry White was the first black American congressman. It is likely that Johnston met both men on his travels to the United States and personally invited them to lecture through the province on behalf of ABA churches. Robinson, who was away on personal business in Boston at the time of the fundraising event, was supposed to get twenty-five percent of the funds collected for the church, although he was not permitted to receive his normal salary while he was away. The Halifax fundraiser was not successful, raising barely enough money to pay the invited speakers. Expenses from the celebrity visits ruined the chances at profit, so the fundraising effort barely broke even. Yet, Robinson received twenty-five percent of the monies collected. A controversy arose when trustees and deacons suggested that Robinson received his salary while he was away.

When Robinson returned to Halifax on October 25, 1898, he continued his pastoral duties at Cornwallis Street Baptist church until November 8, when he resigned. Robinson did receive a salary for those two weeks, but many accused him of dishonesty and said that the salary received was for the time he was in Boston. The controversy broke in a letter to the editor of the *Evening Mail* on November 17, 1898, written by Peter Mackerrow, who was then secretary of both Cornwallis Street Baptist church and the ABA. Mackerrow accused Robinson of dishonesty and also made other charges. Johnston sent a response to the *Morning Chronicle* newspaper defending his friend Robinson. Johnston stated that because of his own position on the church's finance committee, he was better informed than his uncle (by marriage) Mackerrow, remarking that "the press is no place to wash dirty linen in an affair of this kind."

Johnston's efforts did not help, however, as Robinson stepped down from the pulpit after the controversy. According to Johnston's letter to the editor, "Robinson's problem was one that all pastors of the church faced, that he would not grant favours or bow to certain individuals in the church by overlooking questionable acts." Though it required speaking out publicly against a prominent family member, Johnston still defended those he believed were being treated unfairly.

In the political realm, Johnston was an active member of the Conservative Party. It is commonly believed that he became involved in party politics while at Dalhousie. At the time, the Liberal Party supported racial segregation of schools, while the Conservatives opposed it. Johnston frequently appeared as a stump speaker for the Conservative Party at political rallies, and actively promoted black Conservatism, so much so that he became known as "the Conservative leader of his people." In exchange for professional recognition, his peers expected him to deliver the black vote to the Conservative Party.

Johnston was a protégé of Robert Laird Borden, president of the Nova Scotia Barristers' Society when Johnston was called to the bar in 1900, and leader of the federal Conservatives from 1901 until 1920. The connection between Johnston and Borden was largely a matter of traditional black community support for the Conservatives.

In 1898, juggling church, political, and campus life, James graduated with a Bachelors of Laws degree (LL.B). The graduating class of twenty-five was the largest Dalhousie Law School had seen in its fifteen-year history. Johnston articled with Frank Weldon Russell, son of Benjamin Russell, a professor and secretary of the law faculty. His clerkship ended in March 1900, and he was called to the bar on July 18, 1900, which he later referred to as a "Red Letter Day."

From his early days at Maynard Street School to his years at Dalhousie, Johnston met the people who would shape and help build his brilliant career, and formed the personal convictions that would have him speak out for the disadvantaged.

PROFESSIONAL STEPPING STONES

James Robinson Johnston launched his professional career at the law firm of his mentor, John Thomas Bulmer, a long-time supporter of the black community and friend of the Johnston family. Bulmer was the law librarian during Johnston's years at Dalhousie, and a strong believer in educational opportunities for blacks. As such, Bulmer took a leading stance against school segregation during the latter part of the nineteenth century, and was someone to whom blacks turned for legal counsel. Bulmer was perhaps the first lawyer in Nova Scotia to accept blacks as clients and to represent blacks in non-criminal matters. He likely met Johnston before he entered Dalhousie College and certainly would have taken a close interest in his career.

In 1901 Bulmer died, and Johnston took over his law practice and office opposite the Nova Scotia legislature on Hollis Street. As a barrister, Johnston specialized in criminal cases. However, he also handled property transactions and a wide variety of other solicitorial matters. His brothers Clarence Harvey and Frederick Charles worked as clerks in his office. As the first black lawyer in Nova Scotia, Johnston was expected to have only black clients and appear in the police court, where blacks were often hailed on minor criminal charges, rather than in the County Court or Supreme Court. Never one to be limited by others' expectations, however, he consistently aimed for high-profile, controversial cases wherein he had to prove his abilities. Not only did Johnston appear regularly in all the courts, but his cases were also frequently reported in the *Acadian Recorder*, a conservative paper published by the wealthy Blackadar family from 1813 to 1930.

Despite the pressures of building a law practice and a growing professional profile, Johnston's family life was blossoming. In 1902, shortly after he adopted his practice,

Johnston married Janie May Allen, a "light-skinned beauty" born in 1882 in Waverley. Janie May was the eldest daughter of George and Sarah Preeper Allen, who moved to Windsor Junction when Janie was young. The Allen family had six children: three girls, Janie May, Bessie and Isabella, and three boys, William, George Burton, and Harry.

Janie's father, George, was a farm equipment mechanic and apple farmer in Windsor Junction. Janie's paternal grandfather, Rev. Jacob Allen, came to Nova Scotia from Maryland after the War of 1812 and was the first pastor of Musquodoboit Church (now the Guysborough Road United Baptist Church) on Goff's road. The church joined the ABA in 1891.

Janie's mother, Sarah Jane (Preeper) Allen, was the mulatto daughter of Jemima Minnie Preeper; her father's name is not known. According to oral tradition, Sarah Allen was white, a common occurrence in many African Nova Scotian families due to intermarriage. The Preeper family (sometimes spelled "Prepor") was an old family of German descent with deep roots in the Windsor Junction and Fall River area. According to oral tradition, there were both black and white Preepers.

James and Janie met during a picnic organized by the ABA at the Guysborough Road Baptist Church. They were introduced by George Jones, choirmaster at Cornwallis Street Baptist Church, and fiancé of Bessie Allen, Janie's younger sister. Jones had come to Nova Scotia from his native Montreal as a railway porter and soon became active in the Halifax black community. James and Janie courted briefly and were married by Rev. Wellington N. States, a close friend of the groom, on February 26, 1902. Although newspaper accounts report the wedding as held at the bride's residence in Windsor Junction, family lore has it that it was held at the Guysborough Road Church, to which Janie Allen's family belonged. George Jones was best man, and Janie's younger brother Harry Clay (named after the American political leader), aged thirteen years old, attended. Johnston's parents, William and Elizabeth Johnston, and younger siblings were also present.

James and Janie moved to 28 John Street in Halifax's north suburbs. They resided there until 1908, at which time they moved to 25 (now 5559) Macara Street, at the corner of Isleville. In 1910, Janie gave birth to a son by the name of George Henry Stanton Johnston. However, the son died a year later from meningitis. He is buried at Camp Hill Cemetery in the family plot. Although they never had any more children, James and Janie considered their nephews Frank and William, the sons of Bessie and George Jones, as their own, even paying for their schooling. Johnston's nephews attended Maynard Street School, the same school Johnston attended himself. The Joneses lived at 66 1/2 King's Place, just around the corner from the Johnstons.

Family life for the Johnstons was stressful. The death of their first and only child likely created tension within the marriage. As well, Johnston's demanding position as a lawyer and community activist would have meant that he was often absent from the household, going on long trips to visit colleagues in the United States or to different parts of Nova Scotia. Even one of his favourite ways to relax—driving about in a motorcar—took him away from his family.

DISTINCTIVE CASES

After taking over Bulmer's clients in 1901, Johnston built a practice based on a diversity of clients: they were black and white, rich and poor. Indeed, his penchant for controversial cases led him to clients often considered unsavoury by the standards of regular society. It is known that he defended a drug addict in police court in 1902, had charges of rape against a black accused lowered to assault in the Supreme Court of

Nova Scotia in 1903, and appeared as assistant to his former classmate Walter Joseph Aloysius O'Hearn (of moot court fame), in the Halifax County Court in 1911.

In 1907, in the longest court martial held in Halifax, Johnston defended a quartermaster, probably W. P. Butcher of the Royal Canadian Regiment, accused of theft. Quartermasters were responsible for looking after supplies and provisions, and Butcher was accused of stealing money and food from the officers' mess. Over the course of months, money had gone missing and was unaccounted for. Johnston was counsel for the accused, who was eventually acquitted on all charges.

Johnston's best known case was *R v. Murphy,* in which he represented James Murphy, a deaf and illiterate Irish immigrant labourer accused of murdering his grandmother-in-law with a sledgehammer. Margaret Brown was killed on March 8, 1914, at age sixty-four. She was found dead in the home that she shared with Murphy and his common-law wife on Bilby Street in North End Halifax, a stone's throw from Johnston's home on Macara Street. The case was front-page news in Halifax, which is likely how Johnston found out about it and how he came to offer Murphy his services. This was his only known capital case.

The preliminary hearing began March 10, 1914, and lasted five days. The purpose of the preliminary hearing was to determine whether there was sufficient evidence to bring Murphy to trial on charges of murder. There were no witnesses to the crime, but circumstantial evidence pointed to Murphy; for example, he could not account for his whereabouts at the time of the crime, and was considered the scapegoat for trouble in the household. Known to be a violent man, Murphy might also have been mentally challenged—and he did not get along with his mother-in-law. He had motive, opportunity, and perhaps even inclination.

Johnston petitioned the magistrate to give Murphy a longer than normal preliminary hearing, but his plea was rejected. Murphy's life was on the line and the defence needed as much time as possible to examine the Crown's evidence. Johnston sought an additional three days to prepare a proper defence, but his motion was rejected. Johnston also argued that because of press coverage, selecting an unbiased jury would be difficult. Since it would be impossible to get his client a fair trial, he argued that the case should be dismissed; moreover, there was no solid evidence against Murphy. At the time, it was well known that Murphy was a drunk—hardly considered a "respectable" member of the working class—and lived with the murdered woman and her granddaughter, his common-law wife. The grand jury returned a verdict of indictment for murder and Murphy was committed to trial in the Supreme Court.

The trial began on March 30, 1914, and was presided over by Judge James Johnston Ritchie. The defence relied on the overall lack of credibility of the Crown's witnesses, of whom there were sixteen in total, and the sheer circumstantiality of its case against the accused. The first witness was Annie Brown, Murphy's common-law wife and the mother of his two children. Brown clearly believed Murphy was guilty. Johnston pleaded the spousal privilege rule, arguing that Annie Brown should not be allowed to testify against Murphy because they were living common-law. Johnston was overruled, however, on the grounds that Murphy and Brown were not legally married. Before the jury deliberated, Johnston claimed before the packed courtroom that he could positively prove his client's innocence, and gave this striking observation: "The road from the dock to the scaffold leads by way of the jury box." The defence rested its case, calling no witnesses and offering no evidence.

Johnston's strategy of placing responsibility for Murphy's possible execution on the jury's shoulders did not sit well with the presiding judge. Ritchie emphasized to the jury the need to look beyond Johnston's silver tongue, cautioning them to simply weigh the evidence in the case and listen to both sides. As quoted in the April 1, 1914, *Evening Mail*, the judge said to the jury:

Before proceeding any further, I want to make some remarks regarding the address of the counsel for the defence. This was a decidedly clever, ingenious and well delivered argument and reflects great credit on the counsel, but it is my duty to make some criticisms on it. He appealed to you to restore this man to his children and send him back to be a good citizen. This man's plight is undoubtedly pathetic, but that is not a matter for your consideration. You have nothing whatever to do with that, you must confine your attention to determining whether he is innocent or guilty. I do not think it necessary to say anything in reference to "possible judicial murder," and other similar terms used by the counsel for the defence, nor do I criticize the counsel for using them. He has to fight with whatever weapons come into his hands, to fully discharge his duty to his client.

The jury deliberated for almost six hours, but could not reach a unanimous decision. A hung jury necessitated a new trial, and one was ordered for October 1914.

At the second trial in October before Justice Arthur Drysdale, the same witnesses were called. Again, the defence called no witnesses or offered any evidence. Johnston was equally eloquent in the second trial, again using the Crown's evidence to disprove the Crown's case. His cross-examination of Crown witnesses proved positively that his client could not have committed the crime. The jury deliberated for two hours and returned a verdict of "not guilty." Johnston earned the praise of the presiding judge and was even kissed on the cheek by his client Murphy.

Johnston often acted for the defence in cases brought by the Nova Scotia Society for Prevention of Cruelty, as well as in criminal cases involving domestic violence and incest. One such case was *R v. Ward* in 1914, in which John Ward of Halifax was charged with incest on his daughter. The Crown's case centred on the testimony of the manager of the hotel where the alleged incident took place. The manager had heard strange sounds indicating a struggle in the room where father and daughter were staying. The police were called and Ward was arrested and ordered to appear in court. Johnston, acting for the accused, argued that since only circumstantial evidence existed against his client, the charges against him should be dropped. However, the county court judge found the accused guilty. Johnston appealed the conviction of his client to the Supreme Court in Banco (the appeal court). Ward lost his appeal and Johnston petitioned for leave to appeal to the Supreme Court of Canada. (Either the petition was rejected or he was killed before it could be acted upon.) This was an especially difficult case, and the only major criminal case Johnston lost in his career. It attracted much attention and was widely reported in the newspapers.

On the whole, there is no doubt that Johnston was an eminently successful lawyer. His distinction, and the degree of respect he commanded in the courts, shone through in the remarks Nova Scotia Barristers' Society made after his death:

His career at the Bar has been distinctly creditable to him and to the profession of which he was an honored member. His uprightness of character won the confidence of his clients whose interest he ever served with untiring industry and thorough efficiency.

As a Barrister of the Court his modest and gentlemanly bearing, his courtesy to opponents and deference to the Bench won for him a high place in the esteem of the Bench and Bar. On the various occasions on which it became his duty to appear in Court as Counsel he acquitted himself with great efficiency and exhibited a degree of ability and knowledge of his profession which elicted on the very important occasion of a trial for a capital crime the warm commendation of the presiding judge.

The scope of Johnston's legal practice was by no means limited to Halifax. Rev. Wellington States, a prominent African Baptist minister and Johnston's close friend, procured clients for Johnston from across the province. States was the ABA field missionary who traveled throughout the black communities, and he helped Johnston establish a province-wide reputation. As secretary of the ABA, moreover, Johnston had to travel to many parts of Nova Scotia and this also helped him to build a reputation as a lawyer among black people outside of Halifax.

In December 1909, for example, Johnston traveled to Yarmouth, Nova Scotia, to help Mabel Smith search land records. Smith wanted to find the land records of Barbara Cuffey, her great-grandmother. Cuffey was a former slave who had immigrated to Liverpool, Nova Scotia, from Plymouth, Massachusetts, but her land was forfeited when she returned to the United States after the War of Independence. It is unclear whether the records were ever found, as no client files of Johnston's law practice exist.

Johnston also traveled to the United States as an unofficial ambassador for the ABA, and often recruited black clergymen for churches in Nova Scotia. Johnston believed that American-born preachers were better educated and more progressive, and thus more capable of drawing the large numbers needed to sustain a church. Always seeking to improve the well-being of the black community, Johnston poured his time and energy into church affairs, and well as other black cultural activities.

In addition to education and social services, Johnston believed in mobilizing blacks for cultural events that developed race pride. Johnston himself played the organ and in 1902 became president of the Aetna Club, a black musical organization that met at the Oddfellows' Hall on Gerrish Street. In 1904, Johnston served as secretary of the Coloured People's Celebration Committee, which was formed to mark the fiftieth anniversary of the ABA. The celebration was to be based on the 1897 diamond jubilee of Queen Victoria's accession and was supposed to be an annual event to bring African Nova Scotians together to help build solidarity. The celebration on the Halifax Commons was front-page news on July 1, 1904, in the *Acadian Recorder*. Photographs of Rev. A. W. Credit of Philadelphia, one of the guest speakers, and Johnston appeared in the newspaper.

The Colored People's Celebration was never repeated. The African Baptist Church was internally divided along congregational lines, sometimes even within congregations, and between conservatives and progressives. As well, not all black Baptist churches belonged to the ABA. Ever the visionary, Johnston was aiming at a provincial association for the advancement of black people, five years before the NAACP (National Association for the Advancement of Coloured People) was founded in the United States and forty years before it was founded in Nova Scotia.

Johnston also networked through his involvement with a number of Halifax's fraternal societies, such as the Order of Good Templars, the Freemasons, and the Oddfellows, Manchester Unity. Members socialized among themselves, practised and promoted ritual and ceremony, held church parades, sponsored community events like picnics, assisted individual members down on their luck, and undertook some social work within the community, especially in relation to underprivileged children. Well respected among whites, these societies often included leaders of the black community. Membership promoted racial pride and community development. Though blacks were usually excluded from white organizations, they formed their own along similar lines. High office holding in a lodge or friendly society was a source of prestige.

Different racial rules applied to elite professionals like Johnston, however. By 1900, Johnston had become the District Chief Templar for the Independent Order of Good Templars, the highest position in that organization in the city of Halifax. In 1902, he became a member of the Loyal Wilberforce Lodge, an all-black lodge, in the Independent Order of Oddfellows, Manchester Unity, and was appointed secretary. The Oddfellows Hall was located in the heart of the black community on Gerrish Street.

In 1904, Johnston joined Union Lodge, an all-black masonic lodge, where Peter Mackerrow once served as master. Among the members of his lodge were also Johnston's cousin Aubrey Mackerrow, and his uncle, William B. Thomas. By 1906, Johnston had become master of Union Lodge, representing them at the Masonic fair, the gathering of Masonic lodges throughout the province held at the Halifax Armouries. Johnston's energy boded well for his influence within such societies. As Peter McKerrow wrote shortly after Johnston became Worshipful Master of Union Lodge:

Brother J. R. Johnston, a young man in full bloom of health… enters upon his duties at once with many characteristics in marked contrast to those of his predecessors who have had the pleasure of sitting in the oriental chair as Master of the Lodge.

The resolute, aggressive and enthusiastic nature of our young Master should infuse increased energy among the younger members of the Lodge, conceiving himself called upon to lead in a high[er] and loft[ier] scale of Masonic atmosphere [than] ever before attained.

After Mackerrow's death in 1906, Johnston nominated his cousin Aubrey Mackerrow, Peter's son, to serve as secretary. Johnston was influential enough to have his choice selected; unfortunately, it backfired. By 1914, Mackerrow's work as secretary was under review by the Grand Lodge, because by failing to record the minutes of each lodge meeting, he was not meeting his responsibility as secretary. In November 1914, Johnston wrote to his cousin "Mac," telling him what the members were saying about his inexperience, and offering to help him in any way, but it was too late. In April 1915, the lodge's charter was suspended; it was withdrawn in April 1916. There would not be another black Freemasons' lodge until 1948.

Johnston became secretary of the ABA in 1906 upon the death of his uncle Peter Mackerrow. In this important leadership position in the black community, he continually urged the association to work towards meaningful change. As he wrote in the ABA's 1907 Annual Session minutes:

Now brethren, what are you doing? Too often in the past has the charge been laid at our doors that we talk well at the Associational meetings and then go to our homes and do nothing. Let this state of affairs exist no longer. We expect and must have your prayers for the success of the movement. More than that you must contribute to the convention funds so that the work may be carried on.

In 1908, he came up with the idea of building an educational and industrial school for black youth. In Johnston's travels to the United States, it is commonly believed that he traveled as far south as the Carolinas and may have even met Booker T. Washington, the most influential American black leader of his time, and founder of the Tuskegee Institute, the innovative skills-training facility for blacks in Alabama.

The school of Johnston's vision was to be modeled after the Tuskegee Institute, which opened in 1881 and developed into a vocational training school for blacks, giving them the skills they needed to find employment. These included basic literacy and numeracy, training in scientific agriculture, and skilled craftsmanship. Johnston firmly believed in the importance of formal education, as he had prospered from a good education himself. In the same letter from the ABA 1907 minutes quoted above, Johnston writes about the value of education:

The advantages of education cannot be over-estimated. The boys and girls of today are the men and women of tomorrow, and must sooner or later be called to fill our places. Let us see to it that they will have that religious and educational training that will thoroughly fit them for the duties they must assume, and not only be a credit to themselves but to you for the interest you manifested in their welfare.

Johnston was well aware that most blacks living in Nova Scotia at the time did not have the same opportunities he did. By creating such a school in Nova Scotia, he believed that he would give black youth more opportunities than what the racially segregated Nova Scotia school system then provided. Due to economic hardships, black youth were often forced to sacrifice an education in order to provide a subsistence income for their families. The primary objective of the school was to give blacks vocational and technical training that would allow them to move away from the common labour jobs that were often the only jobs available to them. The Tuskegee Institute and other American schools like it were popular and successful in helping blacks. These and other factors influenced Johnston's decision to approach the ABA with the idea.

Johnston also thought that his proposed school could also be used as a shelter for abandoned and orphaned black youth. Sometimes, having an extra mouth to feed was too much for already struggling families to bear, and the abandonment of children became a widespread problem in late nineteenth- and early twentieth-century Halifax. To compound the problem, only a few facilities cared for abandoned and orphaned children, and none of them allowed or accepted blacks. Municipalities placed abandoned black children in poorhouses and similar institutions, where a black orphanage would have been a much better alternative for these disadvantaged children. Already disenfranchised, blacks struggled to build a basic social infrastructure; black orphanages were simply beyond the scope of what the community could sustain. Though the community did what it could to care for its own, the problem was overwhelming. Johnston, having witnessed such tragedies first-hand, decided that something had to be done to improve the situation of abandoned black children. He struck upon the idea of having the proposed training centre double as a shelter for these children.

In 1909, Rev. Moses B. Puryear of Harrisburg, Pennsylvania, joined the cause of improving educational opportunities for black youth. Puryear, the pastor at Cornwallis Street Baptist Church, had likely been recruited by Johnston on one of his many trips to the United States. Puryear was a protégé of Booker T. Washington, and as result found an ally in Johnston. Johnston and Puryear worked hard to bring their idea to fruition, although it was delayed several years.

In 1914, Johnston and Puryear proposed their idea of a black educational and industrial school to the Nova Scotia Legislature, and the matter was listed for debate. In order to gather additional support, Puryear addressed the members of the Halifax Board of Trade. Support for the idea started to build, and it seemed that Johnston's dream was on its way to becoming a reality. But World War One, which began in August of 1914, intervened and progress on the proposal slowed.

Johnston's partisan involvement with the Conservative Party was also starting to gain momentum. Days before the provincial election in June 1911, a group of white members of the Liberal Party interrupted a night school for black children in Preston. The group entered the school, disrupting a class, and offered the teacher, John Scott, a drink of liquor. They also showed the liquor openly to the children present. Scott declined the offer of liquor and protested against their drinking it in front of the children. It was well known that Preston was a Conservative enclave, and this disruption was considered a display of politically motivated racial harassment. The Liberals may also have wanted to embarrass Johnston and discredit his grip on the politics of Preston.

A meeting was organized the night after the incident took place. Johnston was present and gave a strong address denouncing the conduct of the Halifax men who had broken up the class, saying that it was a shame that these men drank and showed liquor openly to the children and that the only reason this occurred was because the children were black. Johnston lodged a formal complaint with the Superintendent of Education and asked for a government investigation. Scott also spoke that night, urging black voters to join sides with the Conservative Party and show their anger towards the government at the ballot box. The Conservative Party at this time was in opposition and the election was only days away. But the Liberals won the election, and no Conservative candidates were returned in Halifax County. During Johnston's time, the Conservative Party did poorly in the polls provincially, and failed to win a seat in Halifax County. The Conservatives were the party of the Confederation, a fact that also hindered them in Nova Scotia.

A few years later, Johnston seems to have considered running for alderman in Ward 6 in Halifax. Ward 6, which included

Africville, had a large black population. Johnston's popularity among blacks and whites alike was very strong, and if given the opportunity, he likely would have won the election. Johnston would not have turned down the nomination, as his father did in the 1890s, as municipal politics could have been the springboard he needed to get into provincial or even federal politics. Other lawyers of Johnston's time proved that law and politics mix well: while Johnston was in university, Halifax lawyer Sir John S. D. Thompson became prime minister; while he was at the bar, another Halifax lawyer, Robert Borden, became prime minister. His association with Robert Borden, and other prominent local politicians, gave him a good chance of advancement.

Between his dream of the industrial school, which looked to be turning into a reality, his political potential, and his active high-profile law career, Johnston was truly becoming a force to be reckoned with. Always intent on improving the situation of his people, Johnston's brilliant ideas and wide-ranging community connections had the power to change significantly the status of black Nova Scotians. However, the events that unfolded on March 3, 1915, put an abrupt end to his seemingly limitless potential.

AN ABRUPT END

In December 1914, Johnston was well-established in his law office on Bedford Row, and the family was still living at 25 Macara Street. James and Janie were joined at their home by Janie's youngest brother, Harry Allen. Harry was working as a stableman at the Exhibition grounds, a job he secured through the help of Johnston. In early 1915, relations in the Johnston household became strained. In February, Johnston and Janie took a trip to the United States, visiting Boston, Norwich, Washington, Philadelphia and Baltimore. A letter

Johnston wrote to George Latimer indicates that Johnston and Janie had met Latimer in Boston and also visited Rev. Dr. J. F. Robinson, who was then pastor at Mount Calvary Baptist Church in Norwich, Connecticut. Meanwhile, Harry Allen had a visit from his girlfriend, Inez Hagen, at the Johnston residence. Janie found out about this visit upon her return, and objected strenuously. A confrontation with her brother ensued, becoming so heated that Johnston had to intervene on his wife's behalf, as it seemed that Allen was going to hurt Janie. To complicate matters, Johnston's younger brother, Albert, had also dated Inez, who chose to be with Harry Allen instead. Additionally, Allen had lost his job at the Exhibition grounds on account of drunkenness. Allen was suddenly left with no job and much animosity towards his brother-in-law. He made plans to leave town for his parents' home in Windsor Junction, where there was plenty of work to be done on the farm. However, Allen delayed his departure from the city an extra day, in order to be present for his sister Isabella's birthday party on March 3.

According to an unknown diarist writing in his copy of *Belcher's Farmer's Almanac*, the day of March 3, 1915, was a cool, dull day, with light snow. On the evening of March 3, Allen returned to the Johnstons' home at about 5:00 p.m. Johnston was expected to arrive later that evening from his Bedford Row office. The Johnstons had planned a family dinner to celebrate Isabella's birthday. On the way home, the lawyer met his cousin Aubrey Mackerrow, whom he invited to attend his lecture the following evening at Cornwallis Street Baptist Church concerning his recent trip to the United States. Johnston arrived home at about 6:00 p.m and instructed Allen to go upstairs and wash for dinner, while he and Janie discussed the events of the day. Allen, subdued from the recent confrontation over Inez Hagen, did as he was told. The doorbell rang, announcing the arrival of clients on business. Johnston left the kitchen and had a brief conference with them in the hallway while Janie stayed in the kitchen. Janie's family arrived shortly thereafter. The family party included Janie's sisters Isabella Allen and Bessie Jones, Bessie's two sons William and Frank, and Emma Allen, Janie's sister-in-law. They proceeded past the clients in the hall to the kitchen, where Janie was preparing dinner.

When finished talking with his clients, Johnston sought a quiet moment in the dining room to read the *Acadian Recorder*, smoke his pipe, and play a game of solitaire. Shortly after the dinner guests arrived, Allen went downstairs to the kitchen through the dining room. After telling everyone he had forgotten his pipe in the living room, he went through the kitchen and back into the dining room, where Johnston was sitting at the head of the table opposite the kitchen door. As Allen entered the dining room, Johnston could be heard saying, "My God, Harry, don't shoot me." After a pause, two gunshots were heard. Both bullets struck Johnston and wounded him, though not seriously.

Upon hearing the gunshots, the three women and two children fled the house, using the shortcut in the backyard leading to Bessie Jones' house in King's Place. Janie instantly thought that Harry had shot her husband. Over the previous three months, tensions between her husband and her brother had escalated dramatically. Not wanting to leave her husband, Janie barricaded herself behind a locked side door to the alley at 23 Macara Street, the residence of Edward Toone, a neighbour and friend of the family. She wanted to stay as near as possible to her husband while keeping a safe distance from Harry.

Next, Johnston was seen pursuing Allen out of the house, through the back door in the kitchen. The two ended up in the front yard of 23 Macara Street. Allen regained control of the weapon, which apparently Johnston had managed to wrest from him, and threw Johnston violently onto the ground, shooting him three more times, once in the mouth. Johnston died instantly. Allen even tried to strangle Johnston, not realizing that he was already dead. Seeing the struggle, a neighbour tried to separate Allen from the corpse. Allen let go of the body and punched the neighbour. Having discharged five of the seven bullets, he left the gun lying in a pool of blood near Johnston's head.

James R. Johnston had been violently murdered at the hands of his own brother-in-law. The black community of Halifax was turned upside down.

Johnston's funeral was on Sunday afternoon, March 7, 1915, at Cornwallis Street Baptist Church. As many as ten thousand people from all walks of life attended the funeral. During the service, Johnston's body lay in state and there were many invited speakers. The first was Edwin D. King, K. C., president of the Nova Scotia Barristers' Society and a trustee of Cornwallis Street Baptist Church.

Next to speak was Dr. John Forrest, president of Dalhousie College during Johnston's student days, and a friend of the family. Many telegrams were read during the service, including one from Prime Minister Borden. Rev. William Harvey Goler, after whom Johnston's second youngest brother was named, also sent a telegram expressing his condolences. Goler, president of Livingstone College in Salisbury, North Carolina, had left Halifax in his youth, becoming a prominent clergyman in the African Methodist Episcopal Zion Church.

The service was conducted by Rev. Moses B. Puryear, and lasted about an hour. Following the service, a funeral procession moved from the church to the Johnston family plot at Camp Hill Cemetery. The funeral procession was led by members of

Johnston's masonic lodge, dressed in full regalia. Along with the thousands of people attending the funeral, it took three carriages to carry all of the flowers to the site of the burial.

Johnston's gravestone reads: "Gone but not forgotten." It also says that he was twice a graduate of Dalhousie University, and a Good Templar, Freemason, and an Oddfellow. Johnston died just days away from his thirty-ninth birthday.

LEGAL PROCEEDINGS

The legal proceedings against Harry Allen began on March 4, 1915. According to the newspapers, large crowds of people arrived at the courthouse on the morning of the preliminary hearing. The promise of a sensational trial drew people to witness history in the making. Though jury trials were not uncommon, murder trials were infrequent events, especially those involving public figures.

Harry Allen appeared in police court on arraignment for the murder of Johnston. Allen, who had no legal representation, confessed to killing his brother-in-law. The preliminary hearing on March 11, 1915, lasted about two hours. Many witnesses were called to the stand, among them Dr. William Finn, who conducted Johnston's autopsy, and F.W. Christie, the civil engineer who drew a plan of the house the day after the murder (see Appendix, p. 71). The other witnesses were Janie Johnston, Bessie Jones, and Edward Toone, the neighbour who had tried to separate Allen from Johnston's body. Neighbours Earle Conrad, C. Mcgillivray and Bill Murray were also called, each claiming to have heard something on the night of the murder. Frank Hanrahan, the city detective who arrested Harry Allen, was also called to the stand. To the utmost disappointment of the spectators, the courtroom was cleared when Janie Johnston requested that her testimony be given in camera. James Terrell, representing Allen, did not object. After

Janie's testimony, the public hearing resumed, but because the central facts were not in dispute, Terrell did not cross-examine the Crown witnesses. The grand jury usually rubber-stamped the indictment if the magistrate decided there was sufficient evidence to indict the accused.

On March 16, 1915, Allen appeared before the grand jury. The following excerpt from the Halifax *Daily Echo* commented on the murder and on Judge J. W. Longley's opening remarks:

He had another case to present to the Grand Jury, which was of grave and important interest. At the last term of the court and many previous ones, James R. Johnston, barrister, was to be seen and heard in several important cases. This term, however, he was not present, as he had been murdered by one Harry Allen. After going briefly over the depositions, the judge remarked that it was lamentable that such an appalling crime had been committed in Halifax. There was no question about finding a true bill, as the accused admits that he shot Mr. Johnston. The case was simply one of murder, pure and simple, and he directed the jury to find an indictment for that crime.

The grand jury did as they were told and approved the indictment against Harry Allen for the murder of Johnston. Allen entered a plea of not guilty by reason of self-defence and a trial date was set for March 25, 1915.

The murder trial lasted one day, purportedly one of the shortest murder trials on record in twentieth-century Nova Scotia. It ran from 10:00 a.m. until 4:20 p.m., with a break of less than seventy-five minutes for lunch. The public was not allowed to view the trial; only court officers and witnesses were permitted in the courtroom. Alfred George Morrison, a senior Crown attorney, led for the prosecution, while the defence was conducted by James Terrell, who had also represented Allen at the preliminary hearing. To the witnesses at the preliminary hearing was added Dr. John Corston, the crime-scene physician who had been dispatched to 25 Macara

Street. The defence offered no witnesses except the accused himself, Harry Allen. In view of the strong evidence against Allen, the defence had few options, so their only strategy was to claim that Allen had killed Johnston in self-defence and to plead mitigating circumstances in Johnston's treatment of his wife. To substantiate this theory, James Terrell put Janie on the stand, where she stated under oath that Johnston had physically abused her. Allen's story of self-defence, combined with his sister's testimony under oath, strengthened the defence's case. Murder began to look like manslaughter. Johnston's character, not Allen's crime, now determined the outcome of the case. James Terrell remarked on this phenomenon in a letter to the Minister of Justice after the trial:

The deceased was an exceedingly popular man in Halifax and more especially because I understand, he was the only coloured Barrister in Canada. Until after his decease, nothing was known of his private life, but upon investigation it appeared that in private he was of a very violent disposition and used to strike and swear at his wife, the prisoner's sister, in a most heartless and disagreeable manner. At the time he was killed the papers here were continually eulogising the deceased and referring to the accused as "the self-confessed murderer."

Nevertheless, the prosecution asked the jury to discredit the self-defence theory, in view of the fact that Allen had shot his victim five times at point-blank range—far exceeding that required to defend himself against an armed man. Both the prosecution and the defence rested their cases. In his charge to the jury, Judge Longley told them to consider three outcomes: murder, manslaughter or acquittal. The judge's failure to distinguish clearly between the first two, however, would prove problematic later.

The jury took twenty minutes to find Allen guilty of murder. Following the decision, it came to the attention of the court that one of the jurors left the courthouse during the lunch break. The juror was Samuel Kent, captain of the tugboat *Gladiator*. Captain Kent's absence gave the defence grounds to appeal the jury's verdict—consequently, the appeal court ordered a new trial.

When proceedings resumed on March 29, 1915, A. G. Morrison, the crown prosecutor, filed a motion for sentencing, while the defence requested that the verdict be overturned. Terrell argued that his client Allen should have his conviction for murder reduced to manslaughter because of the absent juror and the judge's failure to explain to the jurors the difference between murder and manslaughter. Terrell went a step further, arguing that the judge's instructions misled the jury and that a new trial should be ordered. The judge granted Terrell's first motion, that the absence of the juryman did invalidate Allen's conviction, but he refused the other motions.

Terrell appeared in the appeal court on April 9, 1915, and argued for a new trial for Allen on the grounds that the trial judge did not clearly distinguish between murder and manslaughter. The appeal court set aside the jury's verdict and ordered a new trial.

MURDER VS. MANSLAUGHTER

THE CHARGE OF MURDER WAS MADE FOR DELIBERATE UNLAWFUL KILLING, WHEREAS MANSLAUGHTER IS UNLAWFUL KILLING WHICH IS NEITHER INTENTIONAL NOR DELIBERATE. IN LEGAL TERMS, THE PRESENCE OR ABSENCE OF MENS REA ("GUILTY MIND") OR PREMEDITATION DISTINGUISHES THE TWO. CONVICTION FOR MURDER MEANT A SENTENCE OF DEATH, WHEREAS FOR MANSLAUGHTER IT WOULD HAVE MEANT IMPRISONMENT.

The second trial began on October 6, 1915, and was similar to the previous one in that the same witnesses were called and the trial lasted two days. The Crown's new witnesses were the two detectives who collected evidence in the house and C. H. Climo, the professional photographer who took pictures of the crime scene following the murder. According to their testimony, the two officers were the first to meet Allen on his return to the crime scene after the murder. As for the defence, the chief witness was again the accused himself, Allen, and again the strategy was to put the victim on trial and plead self-defence. When Janie took the stand, Terrell asked her whether her late husband had ever threatened her. She responded, "Yes, he threatened me many times." Showing the Johnstons' marriage in a negative light strengthened the accused's case. Terrell asked the jury to put more emphasis on the troubled relationship between the lawyer and his wife, and put aside Johnston's reputation as a fine lawyer and community man.

For its part, the prosecution countered the assassination of Johnston's character by stating that the victim was in no position to defend himself against such attacks. Both the Crown and the defence rested. The judge gave the jury final instructions, taking care to explain clearly the difference between murder and manslaughter. The jury deliberated for two hours. Not to be influenced by Terrell's strategy of self-defence, the jury again found Allen guilty of murder. Two weeks later, Allen was sentenced to be executed by hanging on January 16, 1916, at Dorchester Penitentiary in New Brunswick.

In the days immediately following Johnston's death, the black community turned against Allen. However, when allegations about Johnston's spousal abuse came out at the two trials, the community took sides with Allen and sympathized with Janie. At the announcement of Allen's date of execution, the black community banded together to try to save Allen from hanging.

[far left] **Rev. James Thomas**, Johnston's maternal grandfather, c. 1870. A native of Glamorganshire, Wales, Thomas succeeded Richard Preston as moderator of the African Baptist Association and pastor of Cornwallis Street Baptist Church.

[near left] **Elizabeth (Thomas) Johnston**, mother of James R. Johnston. Rare tintype; the oldest known image of Elizabeth Thomas, c. 1870.

[middle left] **Elizabeth (Thomas) Johnston**, c. 1890.

[below] **Open-lake baptism** at Lake Micmac in Dartmouth, c. 1890s. Probably conducted by Rev. F. R. Langford, pastor of the local African Baptist congregation (now Victoria Road United Baptist Church). Baptism by immersion was typical of African Baptist churches during James Thomas's period.

a "Coloured" Baptism, Dartmouth Lakes -

[above] **James Robinson Johnston**, c. 1896. Bachelor of Letters graduation from Dalhousie University. Among the earliest known photographs of James R. Johnston.

[top right] **Henry Sylvester Williams** (1869-1911) in the robes of an English barrister, c. 1907. Williams, a native of Trinidad, was the first black person to attend Dalhousie. He was also the founding father of Pan-Africanism and the first black to practise law in South Africa.

[below right] **Rev. Richard Preston** ([c. 1792]-1861), c. 1840. Born in Virgina, Preston was a former slave who came to Nova Scotia about 1816 in search of his mother. Finding her in Preston, east of Dartmouth, where many of the Black Refugees were settled, he assumed the name of the old Loyalist township as his own. Preston refounded the African Baptist Church in Nova Scotia and led it for thirty years.

James R. Johnston's law office 58 and 60 Bedford Row (west side) as they would have appeared 1908 through 1915, when James R. Johnston had his law office in #58. Most of the papers from Johnston's office were stolen or destroyed after his death. Rumours persist in family circles that Johnston's law books remain to this day under "lock and key."

[below left] **Benjamin Russell** (1849-1935), one of the founders of Dalhousie Law School, was a professor of law during James R. Johnston's time as a law student. Johnston articled with his son, Frank Weldon.

[below right] **John Forrest** (1842-1920), c. 1900. President of Dalhousie University in 1885. Forrest played a key role in admitting blacks students to Dalhousie.

[top right] **Bessie Maud (Allen) Jones**, Johnston's sister-in-law, c. 1905. Bessie Jones and her husband George left Halifax for Montreal following the Halifax Harbour Explosion in 1917 and the destruction of their home at King's Place, a cul-de-sac between Macara and Sullivan Streets in Halifax's North End.

[middle right] **George Burton Allen**, Johnston's brother-in-law, c. 1900. Known as "Bert" to family and friends, he was the eldest child of George and Sarah (Preeper) Allen. He died mysteriously in 1916, leaving behind a widow but no known children.

[below right] **Emma Allen** (left); **George Burton Allen** (centre); **Janie May Johnston** (right), c. 1905.

[below] **Rev. Wellington Ney States** (left); **George Jones**, Janie Johnston's brother-in-law (right), c. 1900. States (1877-1927), a prominent African Baptist clergyman, was Johnston's closest friend and collaborator. George Jones, known as "Bush" to friends and family alike, was often mistaken for James R. Johnston. Jones was a porter for many years with Canadian National.

[above] **Janie May Johnston**, c. 1907. Picture probably taken at the same sitting as the one of James R. Johnston in masonic regalia.

[left] **James R. Johnston** in masonic regalia, c. 1907

[below] Johnston was deputy grand master of the all-black **Loyal Wilberforce Lodge**, Independent Order of Oddfellows, Manchester Unity (friendly society), c. 1919.

[near right] **Frank Hanrahan**, city detective, Halifax Police, c. 1914. Hanrahan was the crime scene detective who arrested Harry Allen on the spot when he reappeared following the killing of Johnston.

[far right] **James Terrell** was a Welsh-born Halifax lawyer who twice defended Harry Allen on the charge of murdering James R. Johnston. Terrell was formerly a business lawyer and *R. v. Allen* was his first big criminal case. He was instrumental in having Allen's capital sentence commuted to life imprisonment. Terrell was killed on New Year's Day 1921 when the car he was driving collided with a train at a level crossing.

"Slayer of Johnston takes detective into confidence"

"James R. Johnston, Young Barrister, was murdered last night"

[above] **Bessie Jones** and **Janie Johnston** standing on the verandah of 25 Macara Street, c. 1916. The house still stands at the northeast corner of Isleville and Macara Streets. This picture was taken after Johnston's death, but before the Halifax Explosion that devastated the North End and resulted in severe damage to the building.

[top left] **Elizabeth (Thomas) Johnston David**, Johnston's mother, c. 1920.

[middle left] **Frederick Charles Johnston**, Johnston's youngest brother, c. 1920. Served as a porter with the CNR for many years and was the last surviving of the Johnston brothers. According to oral tradition he was a seventh son and had psychic powers.

[below left] **Harry Clay Allen**, Johnston's brother-in-law and murderer (left); **Edna (Harris) Allen** (right), Montreal, c. 1930. Allen and his fiancée were married shortly after his release from penitentiary in 1929. The couple lived a stone's throw away from Union United Church in the heart of Montreal's black community, "Little Burgundy." They had one child, William, who was ten weeks old at the time of his father's death in 1935.

[above] **Cornwallis Street Baptist Church** is the "mother church" of the African United Baptist Association. On the corner of Cornwallis and Gottingen, the building dates from about 1914.

[above] The first executive committee of the newly incorporated **African United Baptist Association**, 1919: James A.R. Kinney (back left), Rev. Wellington States (back right), Thomas P. Johnson (front left), Rev. Arthur Wyse (front centre) and Captain the Rev. W.A. White (front right). Kinney replaced Johnston as Secretary of the ABA and continued his work with the Nova Scotia Home for Coloured Children.

[below] **Nova Scotia Home for Coloured Children (NSHCC)**. Students and staff of the combined orphanage and school on the day of its official opening in July, 1921. James A. R. Kinney was first superintendent. The original building, unused since 1978, still stands, near the site of the Black Cultural Centre for Nova Scotia.

In the days following the conviction, James Terrell protested Harry Allen's death sentence to the federal Minister of Justice. In his petition, Terrell included letters of support from Rev. Moses B. Puryear, as well as Rev. Joseph Stephens, pastor of the African Methodist Episcopal Zion Church, on the corner of Gottingen and Falkland streets. (Both the Johnston and Allen families were members of Puryear's congregation.) These letters carried significant weight, as each claimed to represent the will of the Halifax black community by asking that Allen's life be spared. One native son was lost, and the community wanted to avoid the loss of another. In his letter, Puryear talked about the standing of the Johnston and Allen families in the community, speaking of both Johnston and Allen as respectable young men.

Perhaps as a result of the community's outcry, on December 31, 1915, Harry Allen's death sentence was commuted to life imprisonment at Dorchester Penitentiary. After eight years in prison, Allen petitioned for early parole. His first request was denied, and he kept petitioning until his request was granted in 1929. Upon release, Allen, who had served only fourteen years of his life sentence, was ordered to report to a parole officer for life. Allen was described as a model prisoner who got along well with the guards and other prisoners; he had no previous criminal record. Moreover, both of Harry's older brothers, William and George, were dead and his elderly parents, George and Sarah Allen, were badly in need of his help on the family farm. Janie Johnston offered to secure her brother work among family and friends in Windsor Junction, so that he could support himself and his parents. All of these factors culminated in Allen's early release in January 1929.

Allen returned to Windsor Junction where he worked on his parents' farm until their deaths, circa 1930. He then moved to Toronto, and worked for the Salvation Army as a labourer for one year before being transferred in 1933 to Montreal, where he worked as a fireman for the same organization. At some point after his release from jail, he married a woman named Edna Harris. One night in 1935, while cleaning up at the fire station, Allen was bitten by a rat that he tried to corner and kill. The bite proved fatal—Allen died weeks later in hospital from hydrophobia (rabies). He left behind a widow and ten-week-old son.

With Allen's unanticipated death in the mid-thirties or early forties, final certainties about the case of James Robinson Johnston will never be known. During the trial, many allegations about the kind of man Johnston had been were raised. The difficulty remains in reconciling these possibilities with the brilliance of Johnston's many accomplishments and goals.

PART III: LEGACY DEFERRED

MANY FACTS ABOUT THE CIRCUMSTANCES of James Robinson Johnston's life and death are unclear; conjecture, theories, and half-truths abound. After the gruesome events of March 3, 1915, many shadowy rumours came to the surface about Johnston's character and the circumstances of his death. Whether or not these stories are true, however, cannot be resolved. The only resolution that can occur is how we respond today to Johnston's life and death. Considering Johnston's significant achievements and focus on improvement for the black community, the central question must be: why has his name not been sustained as a symbol for black advancement?

Sadly, the circumstances and consequences of Johnston's death have always overshadowed the achievements of his life. Because of his premature death, Johnston's contemporaries continued the work he started, and so received credit for it. A key example is the Nova Scotia Home for Colored Children. Though Johnston was the originator of the idea for a black industrial school, he never lived to see his vision come to fruition in the way he dreamed. Momentum was just starting to actively build around the idea of the black industrial school when he was murdered. A month after his death, in April 1915, the Nova Scotia Legislature passed the Nova Scotia Home for Colored Children Act. The ABA followed suit and passed a resolution to recognize the idea. In 1917, Trustees were appointed, a building was selected and a matron, Julia Jackson of Philadelphia, was appointed. Unfortunately, in

December 1917, just days before it was slated to open, the Halifax Explosion destroyed the building where the Nova Scotia Home for Colored Children was located. With no chance of employment in the near future, Jackson returned to Philadelphia and things began to look bad for the project. Rev. Moses Puryear left at about the same time and never returned—he had been one of the longest-serving pastors at Cornwallis Street Baptist Church. After a four-year delay, the Nova Scotia Home for Colored Children finally opened in 1921. Over eighty years later the original building still stands, across from the Black Cultural Centre in Westphal, Dartmouth East.

As a result of Johnston's consignment to oblivion, much of the credit for the school has gone to his contemporary, J. A. R. Kinney, the school's first superintendent. Kinney has a plaque in his honour at Cornwallis Street Baptist Church, mounted by the church and the ABA. Johnston has received no such honour, nor any other recognition from either organization.

Coroner W. D. Finn described Johnston as "a healthy and robust man who could have labored an additional 40 to 50 years." We can only imagine the history of African Nova Scotians if Johnston had lived into the 1950s. With Johnston's connections and abilities, black Nova Scotians might have seen their first QC, magistrate, elected politician, or even judge. This last milestone was not achieved until the appointment of Corinne Sparks to the Family Court, more than seventy years after Johnston's death.

It would take another six decades after Johnston's death for a black municipal councillor to be elected in Halifax, with Graham Downey's electoral win in 1975. It took nearly eighty years before Nova Scotian blacks reached provincial politics: Wayne Adams, who was victorious in the provincial riding of Preston-Porters Lake, also became the first black cabinet minister in Nova Scotia. In 1999, Gordon Earle became the first black Nova Scotian Member of Parliament. Johnston paved the way for blacks to participate in electoral politics in Nova Scotia and throughout the Maritime Provinces, without achieving such distinctions himself.

It is also likely that if Johnston had lived longer there would today be more blacks in the legal profession in Nova Scotia. Johnston would have been a worthy role model and mentor for black youth in contact with him. It was not until 1952 that another native black Nova Scotian was called to the bar. George W. R. Davis was a popular man, especially among those living in the historic black community of Halifax's north suburbs. Davis was eventually made Queen's Counsel. Despite such gains, however, native-born black Nova Scotians are still grossly under-represented in the legal profession.

Despite the fact that Johnston's alma mater is Dalhousie University, accounts of the university's history have neglected him. For example, P. B. Waite's *Lives of Dalhousie University 1818–1925* (1994) makes no mention of Johnston; nor does *A History of Dalhousie Law School* by John Willis (1979). Such accounts tend to concentrate, instead, on the struggle of upper middle-class white women in the nineteenth and twentieth centuries to gain admission to Dalhousie University. Though this may be an important aspect of the university's history, similar attention is due to Johnston, a lower middle-class black man.

No mention was made of Johnston in Dalhousie's written history until the Dalhousie Law School centenary of 1983. Then, in 1991, the James Robinson Johnston Chair in Black Canadian Studies was established at Dalhousie University with a $2.5 million endowment, of which more than $1.5 million was raised. The chair supports eminent black scholars by enabling them to teach, conduct research and work in black communities across Canada. This perpetual, self-sustaining fund also promotes curriculum development, visiting lectures, and a special library collection. The chair honours Johnston's name, but has not reflected the historical importance of his life and career. This is striking because among Johnston's mentors was Benjamin Russell, a founder of Dalhousie Law School, professor, and later judge of the Supreme Court of Nova Scotia.

The first scholar appointed to the James Robinson Johnston Chair in Black Canadian Studies was law professor Esmeralda M.A. Thornhill; she held the chair from 1996 to 2002. The current Johnston professor is Professor David Divine, Faculty of Health Professions, in the Dalhousie University School of Social Work.

Similarly, a full-page history of Cornwallis Street Baptist Church written by senior deacon, Clarence Johnston (Johnston's brother), and published in the Halifax *Mail Star* in January 1971, discusses Johnston's contribution to the church without stating that the author and he were brothers. Perhaps, like many black Nova Scotians at that time and later, even Clarence was too embarrassed by the circumstances surrounding the murder to admit his close personal connection. Perhaps, even after fifty-six years, the memory was still just too painful.

COMMUNITY DYNAMICS

Johnston's scandalous death sent shock waves through a community that has never fully recovered from the murder. In order to deal with the turbulent emotions brought on by the incident, the community simply forgot about him, a process made easier by Harry Allen's trials. The silence of the black community was not necessarily a form of cruelty towards Johnston's memory; indeed, this reaction was triggered by the need for self-preservation.

At the time of Johnston's death in 1915, the black community was negotiating the assumptions and degradations of a racist society. The negative stereotypes which labelled blacks as ignorant, lazy, and responsible for their own misfortunes were gradually being overturned by the promise of a better education system (such as the one advocated by Johnston), the potential of black involvement in local politics, and an emerging black professional élite. Considering the hardships that black settlers in Nova Scotia had overcome just to survive, such advancements in the community, only a few generations later, were remarkable.

The importance of upward mobility in a repressive social environment is argued by historian Judith Fingard, who finds that the Halifax black élite (of which Johnston and his family were clearly members) adopted the Victorian ideal of "respectability" as a behavioural code. Such respectability was integral to black advancement and control over their own fortunes. As Fingard writes:

What set [upwardly mobile blacks] apart from their lesser brethren was not greater wealth or more prestigious occupations but their devotion to respectability. The worthy black citizens of Halifax considered respectability to be the key, not only to their superiority over their rough brethren, but to equality with whites, dignity in status, and justice in the public sphere.

For the generation prior to Johnston's, such respectability was especially paramount. Reminded of the hardships and grave injustices their refugee parents had faced, the black community of the mid-to-late nineteenth century struggled to leave such deplorable conditions behind, and take pride in their own dignity and strength as a community.

The Johnston murder came at exactly the wrong time for the upwardly mobile black community. The hard-won, improved status of Johnston's ancestors was still too freshly minted and easily shattered by black–on–black, intra–family violence. In particular, such crime was silenced in the community—had Johnston been killed by a white person, he would have been considered a martyr. As it was, black–on–black crime reinforced the stereotypical image the black élite was trying so hard to dispel. That the victim had been an exalted member of that élite group only made the situation all the more shameful.

In order to survive as a unified and respectable whole, the black community had no choice but to reject Johnston as a leader. Fingard mentions a comparable case, that of the 1892 school board charge against parent Maud Batters. The charge against Batters, a black woman, was instigated by Maynard Street School principal Jane Bruce, who stated that Batters had used abusive language while in the school. This case upset the black élite, not because Batters had ever been a leader in the black community, but because the black community as a whole was still too vulnerable to being discredited; "their hard–won respectability could not be taken for granted" (Fingard).

In response, the black community banded together to support Batters by discrediting Bruce in order to uphold the integrity of their own members. It was important for the black community to be unified, as its reputation was at risk. The community therefore ousted the troublesome Bruce. Fingard explains:

Not only were the black leaders aware that the Batters' case would confirm racist stereotypes, but they also feared that investigation of their own private lives might reveal charges for drunkedness and wife abuse and reliance on charity and other non-respectable forms of behaviour in their own not-so-distant pasts. Such exposure would damage their self-esteem and discredit Afro-Nova Scotian respectability. They had to counter such an outcome by exaggerating the unacceptable behaviour of Jane Bruce.

In the Allen-Johnston case, there was no easy scapegoat such as Jane Bruce, outside of the community, to band against. To support both men was impossible; therefore, one had to be rejected, and that was Johnston. Johnston was an easier target for the community's disregard—his voice was forever silenced, and he could not speak out against allegations raised against him. As well, domestic violence was especially embarrassing to the community, and publicizing its occurrence among the hyper-respectable élite made Johnston an easy target to despise. Allen was still alive, and could still be saved, so the community—led by Janie Johnston—had to work as a unified whole to redeem his life.

Making details of Johnston's private life public tarnished his image not only in the black community, but in the city and province at large. In doing so, it became politique to consign him to oblivion. Harry Allen, though hardly a hero, could be pitied and understood as a wayward and confused young man who had gone astray, provoked by the offensive Johnston. Johnston's alleged indiscretions were ambiguous, and therefore more likely to taint the overall respectability of the community. The fallen leader, who had once epitomized a community's hopes, became an embarrassment—a taboo subject. Discredit then silence were the only ways to deal with his memory.

It is unclear how the white community at large reacted towards Johnston's death, aside from relative disinterest. However, local businessman Charles J. Gibson wrote the Minister of Justice complaining about the reprieve for Harry Allen:

I cannot understand your decision in the Allen case. I am not an interested party at all but everyone knows he committed a foul brutal murder as one shot would have been sufficient to maim his victim but he kept on shooting firing several shots into an unarmed man. What is Canada coming to? Another U.S., where law is a joke?

Even those distant from the case found Harry Allen's reprieve inappropriate by the standards of the day, and in clear contrast to the brutal nature of his crime.

TROUBLE IN THE HOME: DOMESTIC VIOLENCE

The issue of domestic violence became a recurring theme during the trials of Harry Allen. Johnston's alleged abuse was offered in mitigation of the offence. It is possible that much of what was said by the accused and the deceased's wife was largely exaggerated. On the other hand, it is not impossible that domestic conflict existed in the Johnston home.

The difficult truth of this situation is that domestic violence was not uncommon in Nova Scotia in the turn of the century. The media and legal proceedings from Halifax at the turn of the century report many cases such as abused, neglected, or battered women and children. As the frequency of these reports increased, the public became less tolerant of domestic violence. The once sharply-divided spheres of public and private were increasingly beginning to merge, and what happened to women and children behind closed doors became more and more a matter of public concern.

One avenue for help for battered women and children in Nova Scotia was the Nova Scotia Society for the Prevention of Cruelty (SPC), which began aiding abused women in 1880. In reality, the SPC's power was usually limited to a figurative wrist slap, as it had no legal clout. Based on strongly conservative, even prudish, conventions, and usually advocating separation as the best solution for an abused woman, the SPC at the very least offered a place for women to turn and find outside support, a once unheard-of concept.

There is no proof that Johnston did indeed physically abuse Janie. Janie, in an attempt to protect Allen from a death sentence, could have fabricated the story of domestic violence in an attempt to save her brother's life. Moreover, because Johnston was a black man, the issue of domestic violence could legitimize the negative racial stereotypes of this time. Of course, it is just as possible that Janie's testimony was true, which places Johnston in an equivocal light.

Johnston had witnessed domestic violence first-hand while growing up, due to his parents' own marital problems. Johnston's mother, Elizabeth, had complained to the Society for the Prevention of Cruelty about poor treatment by her husband in 1894. By 1901, each was claiming the other was deceased, though both were still alive. It is possible that this childhood familiarity with abuse set the stage for Johnston's own marital problems. If domestic violence had occurred in the Johnston home, it is reasonable to suppose that there were strained relations between Johnston and Allen, as well as between Johnston and Janie.

However, the murder suggests that other tensions also existed between the two men. According to trial transcripts, Johnston and Allen never got along well. This animosity had fueled the argument weeks before the murder when Johnston confronted Allen about why he had lost his job at the Exhibition grounds, a job that Johnston had helped Harry secure.

Another source of tension between Allen and the Johnstons was Allen's girlfriend, Inez Hagen. When Janie found out about Inez's visits, the argument between her and Allen became so heated that Johnston intervened on his wife's behalf. Apparently, Johnston's intervention angered Allen greatly, only increasing his resentment against his brother-in-law.

All that can be known about what happened behind closed doors before the murder was that Allen's dependence on his sister and brother-in-law led to strained relations. One must also note that domestic violence was a common infraction in this time period. Of course, such facts do not explain, much less justify, Allen's murder of Johnston, for which the true motivations will always remain unknown.

The reaction of the black community had a major impact on Johnston's legacy. Had the community chosen to celebrate Johnston's memory, then his name would be better known than it is today. Instead, the silence around Johnston made him a nearly taboo subject, ignored by the community, instead of a symbol of perseverance in the face of racism. Considering Johnston's quest for improvement of the black community, and his own personal achievements, which were significant within a racist province, the reasons why the community silenced his name and story must be questioned.

CONSPIRACY THEORIES

Because Johnston's murder was so brutal, unexpected, and high-profile, over the years conspiracy theories have circulated within the community. Though they are based on little more than conjecture, they will inevitably arise, and may contain elements of truth.

One such theory suggests that Allen was a hired gun involved in a plot against Johnston. Allen's personal troubles had climaxed around the time of the murder. He had lost his job—his only source of income—and yet he owned and carried a loaded pistol, which was unusual for someone not in the military. Allen had been drinking excessively, and was absent from home the entire day of the murder. Apart from Janie, Allen was the only person with regular, unrestricted access to Johnston, except at his office. Allen's position in the Johnston household and his life situation made him an ideal candidate to play the role of a hired assassin.

Around the time of the murder, there was a power struggle in the ABA, as well as the broader black community. The extended Thomas family, which included Johnston, controlled church politics and held elite positions in the black community for over five decades. The Thomas family held dynastic control over the ABA, as the crucial position of secretary passed to Rev. James Thomas's son-in-law, Mackerrow, and thereafter to his grandson. The secretary was the only officer in the ABA with any real power, because he served continuously and travelled among the churches on behalf of the ABA. It speaks volumes for the intergenerational impact of the Thomas family that Johnston could succeed his uncle as secretary of the ABA. Though Johnston was neither a clergyman nor the son of one, he rose quickly through the ranks, effectively blocking others less "respectable" than himself. Many would have resented the Thomas family domination of the church and the ABA.

Similarly, there is no doubt that Johnston had enemies among envious blacks and racist whites. His detractors in the black community tried to explain away his success by saying that he was a product of white philanthropists who paid for his education and schooling. Some blacks thought such patronage gave Johnston an unfair advantage over them, and some even thought he was too successful, accusing him of acting "too white." The conspiracy, if indeed there was one, might have involved people in the black and white communities who felt threatened by Johnston, the quintessential "uppity niggah." As well, some would have known about Allen's personal troubles, and sympathized with his envy and dislike of his brother-in-law.

As interesting as all these conspiracy theories are, however, they are only speculations in the mystery of Johnston's death. What could have motivated Allen to commit such a crime? Just as mysterious is why Allen was carrying a loaded revolver: Who had given it to him and why?

Uncertain Truths and Afterstories

One insurmountable obstacle to understanding Johnston's death is that certain critical circumstances of the case will never be known. Of primary difficulty is that there are discrepancies among the official court transcripts, the police report, and the oral tradition passed down in the family over the years, concerning the events that took place before and after the murder.

The only surviving eyewitness of the final confrontation between Johnston and Allen was, of course, Allen himself. Was Allen's brutal act really triggered by the impulse to defend himself? In testimony at the second trial, Allen said that when the two men were alone inside the study, Johnston stuck out his tongue at him and Allen responded by making a gesture to which Johnston replied, "Is that so?" Allen then said that Johnston picked up a dining room chair and pursued Allen, who took out his gun and shot at Johnston, rapidly in self-defence. Allen then shot Johnston four more times. Three of the bullets struck Johnston, but one missed. Johnston briefly gained control of the weapon and pursued Allen out of the house through the back door in the kitchen. The final, fatal shot was fired outside, before witnesses.

Meanwhile, coroner W. D. Finn and two police officers arrived at the crime scene. According to Allen's testimony, he said to the coroner "I am the man you are looking for." Finn presented Allen to Detective Frank Hanrahan, who then arrested him and took him into custody.

Allen told the magistrate that an argument had broken out at the kitchen table of the Johnston home, when Johnston made a remark to his wife that Allen did not like. This provoked Allen, and he pulled out the gun and shot Johnston several times. Allen stated to the police that Janie was frantic and fled upstairs from the kitchen, then came back down screaming and left the house. Allen's account does not mention the witnesses who were present, and changes the site of the attack from the dining room to the kitchen. Though she was an eyewitness, Isabella Allen was not called to testify at either trial, for unknown reasons.

Allen also claimed to have boarded an express train to Windsor Junction after the murder, which seems unlikely as he could not have got off and returned to the crime scene in time to meet up with the police and the coroner. As well, his bloodied clothes would have raised suspicion on the train, and the police would have received a report almost immediately. No witnesses could place Allen at the railway station, much less on the train, so it is extremely unlikely that he ever left the area of the crime scene.

According to oral tradition, Allen visited the scared witnesses who fled to Bessie Jones's home at 66 1/2 King's Place, only a short walk through the backyard from 25 Macara Street. Allegedly, Allen knocked at the door of his sister's home and Bessie Jones talked to him from behind the door. Allen said, "It's me, Harry," to which Bessie Jones replied, "Don't shoot us!" Allen responded, "I won't hurt you." Bessie then opened the door, letting Harry into the house. Allen told those present not to cooperate with the police and be silent about the events of that evening. The Allens complied with his request. Because the Allens closed ranks and withheld information from the police, important details about the murder case have never come to light. Evidence went missing, and the exact whereabouts of Harry Allen on the day of the murder remain unknown.

There is a long-standing belief in the black community, especially among older members acquainted with Johnston's contemporaries, that Harry Allen was offered a reduced sentence or freedom in exchange for military service during World War One. The story seems to have originated with

Mabel Johnston, widow of William Rufus, Johnston's second oldest brother, and has since passed down through succeeding generations of the Johnston family.

There is no basis to this conjecture in the official records. Allen was in jail from 1915 through 1929. However, shortly after his death sentence was commuted on December 31, 1915, blacks began to be recruited for the Number 2 Construction Battalion. Both William Rufus and his brother Albert served in the battalion. Some blacks are also known to have served in white, combat battalions. As battlefield casualties mounted, enlistments dropped and compulsory military service began to be considered, the Canadian military was more willing to recruit blacks than it had been before. It was by no means unheard-of, in wartime, for deals to be made with convicts allowing them a reduced sentence or freedom in return for military service. Allen, serving a life sentence and expecting to die in jail, had no other options. Accepting such an offer would have promised a release from jail. Allen was also an expert rifleman who would have been in demand as a sniper.

Had Allen gone overseas as a front-line soldier in World War One, he would probably have done so under an assumed name. He could hardly have served with the Number 2 Construction Battalion, because black soldiers from Nova Scotia, especially those from Halifax and surrounding areas, would have recognized him as Johnston's murderer. However, Allen had especially light skin and could have passed as white among people who did not know him. He could easily have melted into an all-white fighting battalion, thus protecting his true identity and achieving a freedom of sorts.

After the murder, the Allen and Johnston families regarded each other as enemies. It was always believed by the Johnstons that Janie had something to do with her husband's murder, directly or indirectly. Before and after Allen's trials, Janie always defended her brother, causing her to be cut off from the Johnston family. Moreover, the focus of the feud was money. Johnston died intestate and his estate was a financial mess. There were unpaid mortgages on several family-owned properties, for which he was partly responsible. Janie inherited his share of other intestate estates, but also debts from the estate of his father, William, and cousin, Henry. Johnston was the administrator of their estates but, because of his sudden death, they were not settled in a timely manner.

Curious deaths befell many of those who were closely involved with the murder. Allen himself died terribly from hydrophobia (rabies). His girlfriend, Inez Hagen, died from pneumonia months after Johnston's murder, on December 27, 1915, only four days before Allen's scheduled hanging on New Year's Eve. Harry's siblings, William and Isabella, also met untimely ends, disappearing from family records only a few years after the murder. Harry's sister, Bessie Jones, to whose house he fled in the moments after the murder, died in 1933 in Montreal, two years before her brother. Finally, James Terrell, Allen's lawyer during both trials, was killed in a car accident on New Year's Day in 1921. Janie Johnston, the person most affected by the murder, lived the longest of anyone directly connected with it. She died on December 4, 1958, of natural causes.

Janie Johnston never remarried, and lived in her Macara Street home for about ten years following the murder. In 1917, while the house was undergoing renovations due to the Halifax Explosion, she left and returned to Windsor Junction. The following year, George Burton Allen, Janie's younger brother, died and assets were divided among the surviving members of the Allen family. At that time, their parents George and Sarah Allen were both still living. Harry, who was in jail when they died, inherited part of the Allen family homestead, which caused a controversy within the family. George Jones, Janie's brother-in-law, became the business head of the Allen family. He went to Dorchester Penitentiary to get Harry to sign away his interest in the property. None of the Allens wanted Harry to have any of the family-owned land, as it was useless to him in prison. At the time, it appeared Allen would be in jail indefinitely. Going to Dorchester Penitentiary with his black lawyer, Joseph Griffiths, George Jones was successful in persuading Allen to sign over his interest in the family property.

Janie Johnston left Halifax for Montreal in 1928 after turning over her Macara Street home to Joseph Griffiths to help pay off her late husband's debts. In Montreal, Janie was employed as a domestic. She returned to Nova Scotia in 1933, when her sister Bessie Jones died, and spent the rest of her life at Fall River. In a letter dated November 12, 1939, to her nephew Robert "Buddy" Jones, Janie Johnston mentioned selling part of her farmland to pay for several trips to Montreal. Age and poor health eventually made travel impossible for her. In her final days, Janie Johnston was in the care of her cousin Martha Preeper Ashe. She died in 1958 at seventy-six. In her will, she gave all her possessions to her cousin Martha. Janie Johnston is buried at Snow's Cemetery in Fall River, in an unmarked grave.

Johnston's mother, Elizabeth, remarried in 1916 to Joseph C. David of Hammonds Plains. By this time, William Johnston had been dead for about six years. Elizabeth (Johnston) David lived in Hammonds Plains with her second husband until his death in 1927. Thereafter, she moved to 1 Gerrish Lane, the home of her son, Albert, where she remained until her death in 1939 in her eighty-second year. Elizabeth David was interred at Camp Hill cemetery in the family plot near son James, first husband William, and grandson George. She was survived by her sister, Inez Thomas, who lived in Shrewsbury, Massachusetts.

William Johnston Jr. (born in 1882), joined the Number 2 Construction Battalion in 1916, eventually becoming a sergeant. When the war ended, he became a porter for Canadian National Railways, like many other blacks in his day. William retired in 1955, and became a guard at the Nova Scotia Legislature. He died in 1966. His widow, Mabel Hill Johnston, who died in 1996 at the age 107, was the last of Johnston's known contemporaries. Mabel Johnston remembered "J. R" well, and often spoke of him.

Clarence Harvey Johnston, also known as "C. H. Johnston," became a station porter in Halifax. In the days following Johnston's death, he replied to Prime Minister Borden's telegram of condolence, requesting a job in the federal public service. The letter has not survived. Clarence was a respected member of the Masons and the Oddfellows, as well as a senior deacon at Cornwallis Street Baptist Church. Upon his retirement, he worked as a security guard for the *Herald* newspapers. He died in 1973 in Windsor, Nova Scotia, at the Masonic Home.

Johnston's third brother, Albert, born 1888, worked as a porter on the railway and in retirement became a cleaner at the Almon Street post office in Halifax. He died in 1964.

Frederick Charles, the youngest of the Johnston brothers, and a clerk in Johnston's office at the time of his death, joined the railway like his brothers. From 1915 to 1962, he worked as a porter. Fred was the seventh son, which, according to lore, bestowed on him the powers of second sight. He claimed to be able to see the ghost of Gerrish Lane, a figure of an elderly woman only he could see. Oral tradition also stated that Fred could heal the sick and see visions. The last of the Johnston siblings, Fred died in 1976.

The rift between the Johnston and Allen families existed for ninety years and has only recently been mended. According to Buddy Jones, who knew many of the principal players on the Allen side, James R. Johnson's murder was a devastating blow to the Allen family. Considered a taboo subject, the events of the evening of March 3, 1915 remained a family secret until the final days of Philomena Amos, Buddy's mother, who died circa 1975. Buddy's father, Francis A. W. Jones, who as a child was present the evening of the murder, carried the burden of what he had witnessed all his life, and ultimately told Buddy about Johnston's murder by "uncle" Harry Allen.

In the Johnston family, the lawyer's memory was preserved to some degree, though his surviving brothers did not talk about the murder itself. For the most part, Johnston's memory has been preserved largely through oral tradition. Few documents survive other than photographs.

LOOKING AHEAD

Johnston's death left a void in the black community of Nova Scotia. Though others such as W. A. White and W. P. Oliver provided important leadership, Johnston's particular emphasis on education over the influence of the clergy was sadly lacking. Johnston had tried to reduce the influence of the

> **BLACK RAILWAY PORTERS** WERE COMMON FROM THE 1880S TO THE 1960S. DURING THIS TIME PERIOD, MOST BLACK MAN IN NOVA SCOTIA WORKED IN SOME WAY FOR THE CANADIAN NATIONAL RAILWAYS. UPPER-ECHELON POSITIONS SUCH AS COOKS, WAITERS, CONDUCTORS, AND STEWARDS WERE RESERVED FOR WHITES UNTIL 1957.

clergy by introducing new ideas, believing that education, not the ministry, should be the path to community leadership. The older, more conservative generation of black clergy and their followers were even in favour of segregation as a means of fostering racial pride. Johnston was a firm believer in integration through education. He believed that the right to lead should be earned, not conferred as a result of being a clergyman. Unknown perhaps even to himself, he set out to undermine the legacy of Richard Preston and his own grandfather. The restored collective leadership saw a return to clerical control over community affairs.

Johnston's story is important for all to reflect upon, as a way to understand both past and present racial attitudes in Nova Scotia. Racial violence can affect black people at any level of society—not just prominent leaders like Johnston or Martin Luther King. Just as slavery produced racism, so racism continues to produce violence, both physical and psychological, against black people. It is essential to reclaim the legacy of James Robinson Johnston as a figure of black achievement in Nova Scotia.

It is also important that Johnston be recognized as the visionary he was. In many ways, he was years ahead of his time. Though Nova Scotia has benefited from many outstanding black leaders, there is always a need for more, for the community—particularly the youth—to identify with. A study, by Maphoka Liphapang of black grade twelve students' perceptions of growing up black in Nova Scotia indicates that greater emphasis on black history is necessary. It is critical for youth to understand black contributions to the Nova Scotia of today. James Robinson Johnston, who achieved much in his short life, is a symbol helping to shape a sense of collective identity and community. As a student from the above-mentioned study states:

I just basically feel…that a lot of young black people like myself who want to go to school would like to learn about their background and their ancestors and their heritage and it has never been given to me and my community…I had to find out on my own that the Citadel building in Halifax was built by black people, no teacher ever taught me that. I mean when Black people are mentioned there is nothing said except that they were slaves…Who wants to hear that?

There is always a need for more black role models to be introduced, or expanded upon, in Nova Scotia's history curriculum. The only way to promote healing is to take away the silence that surrounds Johnston's brutal death, and proclaim the achievements of his life.

The black community was not ready for Johnston, so utterly unique in many respects, at the time of his call to the bar. By 1915, some in the community had had enough of him. For some, Johnston's power, zeal and charisma were such that they were not sorry to see him go. Truly, the manner of Johnston's death was in keeping with his energy in life: both were extreme. There are few Canadian precedents: he was only the second member of the Nova Scotia bar to be shot dead, and he was the only black leader in Canadian history to be murdered.

James Robinson Johnston was a visionary modernist, conforming to neither black nor white stereotypes of black people. He was better educated than the average white person and, accordingly, did not meet the expectations of many whites or blacks. Decades ahead of his time, James Robinson Johnston remains the most controversial and one of the most important figures in African Nova Scotian history.

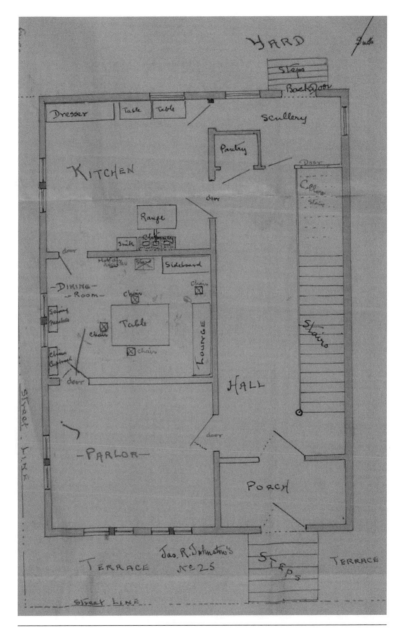

Interior floor plan of 25 Macara Street shortly after Johnston's murder. Drawn by F. W. Christie, a civil engineer, this plan was given in evidence at Allen's trials.

Hon. Minister of Justice
90 Ottawa Ontario
Now
Hon. Sir:— CC/208

    Having served 8 yrs of a
Life sentence I beg to submit my
application asking for my release
under Ticket of Leave or at least
a reduction of sentence.

    I was of a wild nature
and had a tendency to sow wild
oats, if released now I will try to
live an Honorable life in the future

    Stephen Bros of Windsor
Jct. have assured me Employment
if released.

        Awaiting Your decision
    I am, Your obedient Servant
      Harry Allan
       Q 87

Harry Allan
Q 87.

Harry Allen's release request, 1923.

Halifax N.S.
April 24/24

Mr Cochrone,
Dear Sir :—
My brother Harry at Dorchester
asked me to write you
on behalf of him. And he
told me that you were
trying to help him. Dr Gauff
at Halifax here said that
he could get Harry employment and the Stephen
Brothers at Windsor Junction
would also give Harry work
Than he could go to
work on his own father's
farm and father would
build him a modern chicken
house and he would get
him a couple of cows so
that he could work on
the farm as father is

Letter from Janie Johnston, 1924.

too old to worke and there
is plenty of worke to be done
and Mr Cochrone I would
like to see Harry get
his freedom if possible
for the sake of his mother
and father for they are all
alone and he was their
only support
Now I hope you will
write to Ottawa immediately
and inclose this letter if
you think it necessary.
And I hope you will
succeed and please write
me soon.
            Yours truly
        Mrs J. M Johnstone
              2 5 Macara St.

Letter from Janie Johnston, cont'd.

LICENSE

UNDER THE TICKET OF LEAVE ACT.

His Excellency the Administrator of the Government

is graciously pleased to grant to ___Harry Allen No. Q-57___

who was convicted of __murder at Halifax before the Honourable__

__Mr. Chief. Justice Graham,__

on the ___22nd October, 1915,___ , *and was then and there*

Death - such sentence having been on the 31st December,

sentenced to ~~imprisonment~~ 1915, commuted to life imprisonment

by Order-in-Council-

~~~~

and is now confined in the ~~said~~ Dorchester Penitentiary ___, license*
to be at large in Canada from the day of h is *liberation under this order*
during the remaining portion of h is *term of imprisonment unless the said*

___Harry Allen No. Q-57___

shall before the expiration of the said term be convicted of an indictable
offence within Canada, or shall be summarily convicted of an offence involving
forfeiture, in which case such license will be immediately forfeited by law, or
unless the license be sooner altered or revoked.

This license is given subject to the conditions endorsed hereon
and may be revoked for breach of any of the said conditions whether
such breach be followed by conviction or not, or it may be altered or
revoked according to the pleasure of the Governor General. If, however, this license be not altered, revoked or forfeited, or liable to forfeiture for any existing cause, on the day when the above-mentioned
sentence would expire, if reduced by remission earned at the time of
the convict's release, which day will be specified by the Warden, or
other proper officer of the prison, in the margin opposite hereto, then
the said sentence will be deemed to have been satisfied, and this license
will have no further operation or effect.

Date of
satisfaction of
sentence.

His Excellency *hereby orders that the said*_____

___Harry Allen___   *be set at*

liberty within thirty days from the date of this order. __Allen to be released__

__so soon as the Warden is satisfied that suitable employment__

__has been arranged for him.__

Given *under my hand and seal, at Ottawa, the* 12th

August, 1929.

day of   THOMAS MULVEY!

Under-Secretary of State.

Harry Allen's release permissions, 1929.

Montreal Nov. 6ᵗʰ 1934.
Mrs. Harry Allan
3578 Delisle St.
Montreal P.Q.

Dear Sir.

I am writing to you in
connection with Harry he is supposed
to correspond with you every three
months—about his conduct I dont
know what he says. But his
carry on is—disgraceful you cant do
anything with him he—does nothing
but fight from monday morning
till saturday night. I wish you
would send some-one to look into
the matter for you are the only
people he is—a scared of and bind
him over to the peace. He acts-as
if he is not-all there or I dont
know what-ales him. I have been

Letter from Mrs. H. Allen, 1934.

going to write before but he always
says give me another change. He
is imposible you cant go on the
street for him.

Yours Truly.

Mrs. H. Allan.

Hopping to hear from you soon. When
you send to the house because
I can explain the matter. I want
you to scare him because his language
is terible. At least if he knows he
is bound-over to the peace he has
to behave.

Letter from Mrs. H. Allen, cont'd.

The Salvation Army
(William Booth, Founder)

Territorial Headquarters
Canada, Alaska, Newfoundland and Bermuda
James and Albert Sts.   -   Toronto 2, Ont.

August 2nd, 1935.

Mr. M. F. Gallagher,
Chief of Remission Branch,
Ottawa, Ont.

Dear Sir;

    This note is just to inform you that HARRY
ALLEN. Colored man, who has been under our care on
parole for many years, and who has been working on
our premises since his parole, died on July 31st,
1935, and will be buried by TheSalvation Army today. Thus his Ticket of Leave expires.

    I might say that he leaves a wife and ten
weeks old baby.

    The poor fellow has been doing, for the
past years, as well as could be expected, and has
needed our oversight, which, of course, has been
gladly given.

              Sincerely yours,

              (E. Sims - Lt.-Colonel)
              Men's Social Secretary.

Letter from Salvation Army announcing Allen's death, 1935.

ACKNOWLEDGEMENTS

This book was brought to life with the help and support of many people.

First, I would like to thank my family for providing financial support and encouragement since I started working on this project. Without their help, the book would not have been possible.

I am indebted to the many distinguished people who shared their stories and insights with me. I would like to say a special thank-you to Robert "Buddy" Jones, Aletha Johnston Williams, and Rev. Sherrolyn Riley. Each contributed something special and tangible, and I thank them for their time and input.

My sincere appreciation goes to Saint Mary's University, especially Dr. James H. Morrison, professor of history, and Fr. William Lonc S.J., professor emeritus of the physics and astronomy department, for their support and encouragement not only with this book but with other pursuits over the years.

Thank you to editor Zsofi Koller, whose skill and dedication to this book improved it beyond measure.

I would like to thank Professor David Divine, newly appointed James Robinson Johnston Chair in Black Canadian Studies at Dalhousie University, for his support.

Thanks are also extended to the staff of Nova Scotia Archives and Records Management for their research assistance.

Bibliography

Primary Sources: Archival

Johnston v. Johnston et al.: RG 39 "C", box 592, file B-1285, Nova Scotia Archives and Records Management [NSARM].

Halifax County Court of Probate. Estate settlement case file 8040 (James R. Johnston).

RG 39 M box 23 file 6, NSARM (bar admission file)Supreme Court of NS Proceedings Book. Beginning May 13th 1898" at 398 [18 July 1900], NSARM (call to bar).

RG 38 "C" (HX), box 294, file B-61, NSARM (R. v. Ward).

RG "C" (HX) , box 579, file B-265, NSARM (R. v. Ward).

RG 125, vol. 351, file 3501, Library and Archives Canada (R. v. Ward).

RG 39 "C" (HX), box 700, file R-228, NSARM (R. v. Murphy).

Minutes of the Fifty-Fourth Annual Session of the African Baptist Association of Nova Scotia. Halifax: McAlpine Publishing Co., Ltd, 1907.

Minutes of the Forty-Seventh Annual Session of the African Baptist Association. Halifax: McAlpine Publishing Co., Ltd, 1900.

Union Lodge [No.18, A.F & A.M.], records, MG 20, vol. 2218, File 1; vol 2012, file 2; vol. 2130, file 34 NSARM.

RG 13, vol. 1526, file CC 208, Library and Archives Canada (Harry Allen capital case file).

RG 39 "C" (HX), box 700, file R-254, NSARM (Harry Allen murder trial).

RG 39 "C " (HX), box 589, file B-1058, NSARM (Harry Allen murder trial).

RG 39 "A" vol. 51, NSARM (Harry Allen murder trial).

RG 41 D box 82, file 1419, NSARM (medical examiner report on James R. Johnston).

Halifax County Court of Probate. Estate settlement case file 7171 (estate of Henry T. Johnston).

Halifax County Registry of Deeds, book 389, page 389, page 530, no. 456 (1908).

PRIMARY SOURCES: PRINTED

Dalhousie Gazette, Vol. 29. No. 1, October 1896 (Arts graduation).

Halifax *Morning Chronicle*, 15 April 1898, p.6 (Moot Court).

Halifax *Evening Mail*, 21 April 1898, p.1 (Law graduation).

Dalhousie Gazette, Vol. 31 No.1, October 1898.

Halifax *Evening Mail*, 1 April 1914, p.11 (R. v. Murphy).

Halifax *Morning Chronicle*, 4 March 1915 (murder of James R. Johnston).

Halifax Herald, 4 March 1915.

Halifax Herald, 6 March 1915.

Halifax Herald, 8 March, 1915.

Halifax *Acadian Recorder*, 17 March 1915.

Halifax *Acadian Recorder*, 19 March 1915.

Halifax Herald, 29 April 1915.

Halifax *Acadian Recorder*, 6 October 1915.

"The Late J.R Johnston." *Atlantic Advocate*. Vol. 1. No.1 (Apr. 1915).

SECONDARY SOURCES

Abucar, Mohamed. *Struggle for Development: The Black Communities of North and East Preston and Cherry Brook, Nova Scotia, 1784-1987* (Halifax: McCurdy Printing, 1988).

Cahill, Barry. "The 'Colored Barrister': The Short Life and Tragic Death of James Robinson Johnston, 1876–1915." *Dalhousie Law Journal* 15 (1992): 336–79.

Clairmont, Donald H. *Nova Scotian Blacks: A Historical and Structural Overview,* no. 83 (Halifax: Institute of Public Affairs, Dalhousie University, 1970).

Clarke, George Elliott, ed. "Mr Johnston for the Defence." *Fire On the Water: An Anthology of Black Nova Scotian Writing.* Volume One (Lawrencetown Beach NS: Pottersfield, 1991): 82-85.

Fingard, Judith. "From Sea to Rail: Black Transport Workers and Their Families in Halifax, c. 1870-1916." *Acadiensis* 24 (Spring 1995): 48-64.

Fingard, Judith. "Johnston, James Robinson." *Dictionary of Canadian Biography.* Vol. XIV, 1911-1920 (Toronto: UTP 1998): 543-544.

Fingard, Judith. "The Prevention of Cruelty, Marriage Breakdown and the Rights of Wives in Nova Scotia, 1880-1900. *Acadiensis* XXII, 2 (Spring 1993): 84-101.

Fingard, Judith. "Race and Respectability in Victorian Halifax." *Journal of Imperial and Commonwealth History* 20 (1991–92): 169–95.

Foote, Arthur L. "James Robinson Johnston." *Hearsay.* Vol. 8. No. 2 (Autumn 1983): 14.

Fosty, George and Darril. *Black Ice: The Lost History of the Colored Hockey League of the Maritimes, 1895-1925* (New York: Stryker-Indigo Publishing, 2000).

Girard, Philip. "'His Whole Life Was One of Continual Warfare': John Thomas Bulmer, Lawyer, Librarian and Social Reformer." *Dalhousie Law Journal* 13 (1990): 376–405.

Griffin-Allwood, Philip G.A. "The Reverend James Thomas and 'Union of All God's People': Nova Scotia African Baptist Piety, Unity and Division." *Nova Scotia Historical Review* 14:1 (June 1994): 153-168.

Jobb, Dean. "Murdered Promise." *Bluenose Justice: True Tales of Mischief, Mayhem and Murder* (Lawrencetown Beach, NS: Pottersfield Press, 1993): 147-52.

Liphapang, Maphoka Chris. "Growing Up As A Minority in a White Dominated Society: Black Grade 12 Students' Perceptions." Dissertation. 1993.

Morton, Suzanne. "Separate Spheres in a Separate World: African-Nova Scotian Women in Late-19th-Century Halifax County." *Acadiensis* 22 (1992–93), no.2: 61–83.

Oliver, Pearleen. *A Brief History of the Colored Baptists of Nova Scotia, 1782–1953* [1953]; reprinted 1990.

Pachai, Bridglal. *Beneath the Clouds of the Promised Land: The Survival of Nova Scotia Blacks.* Vol. 2, 1800-1989. Halifax: Black Educators Assoc., 1990.

Saunders, Charles R. *Share & Care: The Story of the Nova Scotia Home for Colored Children* (Halifax: Nimbus, 1994).

Sherwood, Marika. "Williams, Henry Sylvester (1869-1911)." *Oxford Dictionary of National Biography.* Oxford University Press, 2004.

Winks, Robin W. *The Blacks in Canada: A History.* 2nd Ed. Montreal and Kingston: McGill-Queens University Press [1971]; reprinted 1997.

Image Credits

Images credits are arranged from top to bottom, left to right on the page.

Archives nationales du Quebec:
B-2

Black Cultural Centre of Nova Scotia:
p. xvi, A-1, A-3, A-4, B-3, D-4, E-2, E-3, G-1, H-1, H-2, H-3

The Bud Jones Historical Collection of Canadian Blacks:
D-1, D-2, D-3, E-1, G-2, G-4

Dalhousie University Archives Photograph Collection:
B-1 , C-2 (PCI, Box 17, Folder 134), C-3 (PCI, Box 7, Folder 2)

Haliax Herald, 3 January 1921
F-2

Halifax *Daily Echo*, 4 March 1915
F-3

Halifax *Morning Chronicle*, 4 March 1915
F-4

Johnston Family Archives:
A-2, G-3

Library and Archives Canada
p. 71, p.72, p.73-4, p. 75, p.76-7, p. 78

Nova Scotia Archives and Records Management:
F-1

Nova Scotia Museum, History Collection
C-1